All Power
Fighting

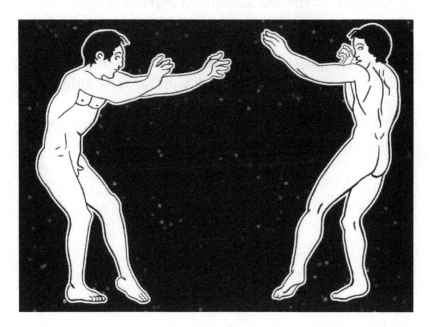

A Fighter's View of Mixed Martial
Arts from Achilles to Alexander

All-Power-Fighting

Dust Cover

All Power Fighting is the third Volume of The Broken Dance is the history of Pankration, of "The-All-Power-Thing" from its earliest inception in Archaic Hellas down to the death of Alexander the Great. Copiously illustrated, the lives and the methods of the ancient mixed martial arts champions are brought to vivid life.

From the perspective of the fighter the martial culture of the ancient Greek warrior is examined, including the war arts of wrestling, dueling, archery, spear-throwing, stone-throwing and the pentathlon—the famed five contests.

Research Assistance: Erika Cooper, Baltimore
County Public Library
Critical Reading: Professor David Carl of Saint
John's College at Santa Fe; Jay Harding
EDS. University of Iowa, kenpo & kali instructor;
Doctor David Lumsden, MMA coach.
Instruction: "Reds" Foley; Ed Jones; "Irish" Johnny
Coiley; Arturo Gabriel; Frank Gilbert; Jimmy Hines;
Dan Funk; Leroy Dinatale

For Travis Ryan LaFond.

This is the third of four volumes that comprise *The Broken Dance: A Fighter's View of Boxing and Prizefighting from Pre-history to the Fall of Rome.*

The Illustrator

Joseph Bellofatto Junior's paintings and illustrations have been featured on the covers and interiors of *Absolute Magnitude* and *Gateways Magazine*, and books by *Quite Vision Publishing*. He won an honorable mention in the L. Ron Hubbard *Writers Artist of the Future* contest. He lives with his wife, children and dogs in suburban Maryland.

The Author

James LaFond lives and works in the "once great medieval city" of Baltimore, Maryland. He has fought 20 submission boxing bouts according to LPR, Gypsy and Greek rules, for 7 wins, 4 losses and 9 draws.

Contents

Introduction

This work is being presented from the fighter's perspective; including the timeless fighter of any culture that might read such a work to glean a glimpse of those who fought in some distant place and time, and—as much as possible—from the specific perspective of the ancient Hellenic warrior. In attempting to study the subject from such a distant and subjective viewpoint one must be particularly careful to consider source material in context. This is most true of the period of Greek martial dominance.

The body of period evidence for the Hellenic combat arts—especially for prize-fighting and athletics—is dominated, and indeed originates, with the works of Homer: *The Iliad* and *The Odyssey*. Modern academics may debate whether or not Homer was the author of both works, if they were history, fiction or both, whether the characters were even patterned on real persons, and, of course, agree completely only on the fact the gods of Olympus were fictitious. However, the fighters of Hellas regarded the works of Homer as history, believed in his poems as much as Americans believe in their *Bill of Rights*, treasured his heroes as Catholics treasure their saints, and believed fiercely in their gods; and, if we are to see combat from their perspective, so should we, for at least so long as we read their words and wonder at their struggles.

The names of Hellenic fighters were constructed to be meaningful and descriptive. We may only guess at whether a particular fighter's name was a fight name concocted by an admiring epigrapher or the gift of a doting parent hoping that a powerful moniker might prove prophetic, or a hereditary name reflecting the characteristics of an admired ancestor*. Whatever the case may be, those of all mythic and historical fighters presented in this book shall be translated, under the assumption that a fighter's name either reflected his character, or effected his character as he sought to live up to that personal title bestowed by those who cared most profoundly about his fate.

The warriors and athletes of ancient Hellas were *all* mixed martial arts practitioners. They engaged in athletics for physical conditioning and often as the keynote of a personal quest for immortality. They all, to a man, practiced the war arts upon which their freedom and the survival of their community depended. The one athletic art that was thought to prepare a warrior to handle the pressure of a battlefield command was pankration, literally all-power-thing. Those who fought in and dominated the all-power-thing at sacred contests were looked to as diplomats and front-line-fighters of small towns, regimental and squadron commanders for independent city-states; and as the personal drinking companions and bodyguards of tyrants, kings and emperors.

These were the supermen of their time, practicing the art of Herakles, mightiest of mythic heroes. When an ancient MMA fighter walked out onto the dug-up [the raked earth of a race-course] to face his opponent, he was also facing the gods, who dared him to survive the agonies of combat in his—usually doomed—bid to take his place among them.

While we, the modern fighter or fight enthusiast, examine their methods, read their stories, and wonder about their accomplishments and their often unknown fates; we would do well to remember that this was, in the final analysis, why they strived so furiously for victory; so that the people of some distant future might remember them.

By remembering them, we are, in essence, raising their hands for their final victory.
-James LaFond, September 30th, 2010, Baltimore Maryland

*This author believes that the names of prize-fighters were predominantly names earned through their athletic or military accomplishments.

A Note on the Illustrations

The figures and maps in this volume are part of a larger study and are numbered according to the entire scheme, and therefore do not start at 1.

A Note on Terminology

A glossary of Greek martial terms is published in By The Wine Dark Sea by the same author.

Figure 24.

Hektor and Achilles Beneath the Walls of Troy

The images of Hektor and Achilles evoked by Homer in *The Iliad* would continue to shape the worldview of Greco-Roman fighters for well over 1,000 years. For the Greeks the image of Achilles as the singular athlete: "breaker of ranks"; and "matchless runner"; who over-came massed warriors and ran down the noble Hektor "as a hound in the mountains hunts a fawn from its lair" would remain the martial archetype, emulated by the greatest athletic conqueror of all time Theogenes of Thasos, as well as the greatest military conqueror of ancient times Alexander the Great. Roman fighters tended to emulate and honor Hektor, the doomed and dutiful soldier, sacrificing everything for his tribe.

War and Agony

The Martial Arts of Hellas from Achilles to Khilon, 1220 to 323 B. C.

> "I'll stand up to the man—see if he seizes glory
> or I'll seize it myself! The war-god is impartial:
> he deals death to the man who deals death."
> -Homer, *The Iliad* [Book 18, *The Shield of
> Achilles*, 358-360]

In the passage above, the Trojan hero Hektor swears to duel Achilles. The words of this simple suicidal oath express the ethos of the ancient hero perfectly: the greatest virtue is to stand one's ground in combat; the prize for victory is an immortalizing form of recognition; and one's virtue and martial artistry shall be judged by an impartial and pitiless force. From the clash of shields on the battle line, to the dance of spears on the dueling ground, to the exchange of blows in boxing, the fighting men of ancient Hellas trained and fought according to this grim code. Their war arts were many, were often brutal, and fell into 3 general categories: *polemakhia* [war-fighting]; *monomakhia* [dueling]; and *athletics* [prize-seeking].

A detailed study of war-fighting and dueling in ancient Hellas is beyond the scope of this book. However, references will be made to these arts, as athletics were intricately related to these practices. *Agonistiks* [athletics practiced in preparation for sacred contests] were engaged in by amateur athletes and citizen soldiers as an imperfect but tolerable preparation for the rigors of mass battle; as well as by professional athletes who would emulate the heroes of the *Iliad* at sacred *agons* [contests]. In short the ancient athlete emulated the duelist as he prepared for the agonies of the contest; contests which had evolved to reflect specific battlefield conditions, either as a metaphor or as a method of practical preparation, and therefore provided the part-time soldier of ancient Greece with a level of physical and psychological conditioning far superior to that of the traditional tribal warrior.

The grim shadow of the Homeric duelist and the bloody battle fields that provided the background for his struggles haunted—indeed dominated—the whole of ancient athletics until the fall of Rome. It was no accident that the greatest athlete of all time, Theogenes of Thasos, gave up boxing for running in his mania to outdo a mythic figure who had been dead for 700 years by the time of his birth—for Achilles had been known as the fastest of men. Many were the ancient prize-fighters who played Hektor to the stark shadow of Achilles as they fought for immortality.

Now, imagine yourself a prize-fighter in a world where one could literally become a god...

Map 7.

*Hellas and Magna Grecia**,

circa 530 B.C.

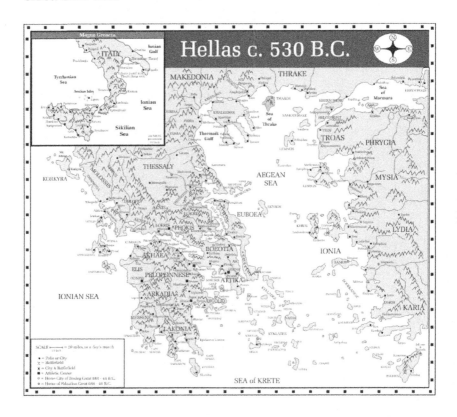

*Magna Grecia is a Latin term meaning "Greater Greece" used to describe the Greek colonies in Southern Italy and Sicily. For a larger copy of this map, be sure to check out *The Gods of Boxing*.

Arete

Martial Virtue from Akhilles to Kallippos,1220 to 332 B.C.

"A man can claim no greater fame
—while he lives—than strength and speed
demonstrated with his own hands and feet."
-Homer, *The Odyssey*

The ancient Greek concept of *arete* encompasses the modern English concepts of virtue, skill, prowess, excellence, valor, nobility and even pride [pride not generally being regarded as a virtue in modern times].* These are the specific martial virtues embodied by the war god Ares. The fact that the preeminent virtues of the Hellenes are the virtues of the warrior says a great deal about the politics and culture of ancient Greece. *Arete* is the underpinning concept that unifies the war-arts of Hellas into an understandable though alien ethos.

19

All war-related activities and sports can accurately be defined as war-arts. However, our discussion in this chapter will focus on those arts that sprung directly from the battlefield practices of the Homeric period of 1220 to 725 B.C.** Those arts that had a relationship to war as a general preparation or martial metaphor, such as wrestling and all-power-fighting, but were not actual battlefield arts important to the winning of battles, are discussed in their proper place, as the main focus of this book. Hellenic war arts are listed below according to their order of appearance in literature, which coincided roughly with their level of prestige throughout the Hellenic period. Those discussed in this chapter are in bold.

Arma [chariot racing] 1st event in Book 18 of *The Iliad*, circa 750 B.C.***

Pugmakhia [boxing] 2nd event...

Pale [wrestling] 3rd event...

Stade [foot race] 4th event...***

Monomakhia [fencing] 5th event...

Diskus [throwing-stone] 6th event...

Toxon [bow] 7th event...

Akontion [javelin] 8th event...

Halma [jumping] *The Odyssey*, circa 725 B.C.

Pentathlon or "five exercises" [discus, jumping, javelin, running & wrestling] *Olympic,* 708 B.C.

Pankration [all-power-thing] *Olympic,* 648 B.C.

Those war-arts which were never ritualized

into sport were either purely technical military arts such as *teikhomakhia* [siege craft or combat-engineering] or concerned the maneuver of soldiers as an arms team. Those war-arts practiced and preserved as sports were individualized in the extreme, and focused on developing and testing the *arete* of the Hellenic martial artist. A male citizen of Hellas was expected to practice boxing, wrestling, running, fencing, stone-throwing, jumping and javelin throwing. The chariot and the bow were for the rich and the barbaric, and the pankration reserved for Spartan boys and high-level combat athletes. All of these 10 disciplines [the pentathlon being a collection of 5 arts] formed a corpus of martial knowledge respected and valued by the warriors of Hellas.

These ritualized contests began as demonstrations of skill in the use of battlefield weapons. Prowess in trials reflecting those attributes most valued among the tribal foot-soldiers of Hellas eventually resulted in the elevation of the *pentathlon* as the premier venue for the demonstration of one's *arete*. Eventually the ideal of the self-cultivated citizen soldier tempering himself for war in small-town athletic facilities, and showing off his prowess at sacred religious sites gave way to the more fanciful, less useful, and thoroughly more brutalized figures of the prize-fighter and chariot-jockey. But between the rustic times of Homer and the world of imperial politics that would finally transmogrify combat sports into something eerily modern, there would be roughly

350 years of frenetically aesthetic martial artistry that would set the fighters of Hellas apart forever.

*Miller, Sephen G. *Arete: Greek Sports from Ancient Sources*, University of California Press, Berkeley, CA, 1991, pages vii-xii

Miller's discussion of *arete* is wide-ranging and insightful, and for a university press book it is a very good read.

**The period defined in this study as "Homeric" spans the period from the supposed date of the siege of Troy—the subject of the *Iliad* [1220 B.C.] to the probable date of the composition of the *Iliad* [750 B.C. and the *Odyssey* [725 B.C.] by Homer. Historians typically define this span as various periods: Mycenaean [1600-1100 B.C.]; Greek Dark Age [1100-750 B.C.]; Protogeometric 1050-900 B.C.; and Geometric [900-700 B.C.]

** The chariot and foot races eventually gave rise to a variety of equestrian and running events [such as horse-racing and running in armor], which are not essential to this discussion and can be appreciated in their ritual context by referring to the *arma* and *stade* events. Note: There were more than 20 Hellenic terms for the horse-drawn car or chariot.

Arma and Hippo

Chariot & Horse

"Achilles' call rang out
   and in answer the fastest drivers surged
forward."
               -Homer, *The Illiad*

It is possible that chariot-racing was the first Olympic sport*, and it is well-known that chariot-racing was the most popular mass-entertainment in the age of Rome. However, the variety of rigs entered in various Olympics and the heavily-financed super-carts of the Roman circus are not important to this discussion. What is of interest for those of us studying the evolution of prize-fighting arts in ancient Greece, is the nature of the war-cart depicted in Homer's *Iliad*.

The Homeric chariot seems to have been of

the light two-horsed variety used by the Minoans. This buggy was easily transported by sea in small ships as a "kit". It was a light, easily crated vehicle somewhat analogous to the U.S. military's jeep of the World War II and Korean War era. Its Roman counter-part was the *biga*, a light civilian transport used for municipal transportation in late antiquity. This is not the 4-horse-power race-car of *Ben Hur*, or the heavy scythed war-cart employed by the Great Kings of Persia. The vehicle in question is a light 2-horse-power rig, piloted by a skilled driver who, if he engaged in combat, only did so as a rescue pilot or as a casualty. What is the significance of such a chariot to the evolution of the combat arts? This apparently trivial question is actually quite important, for boxing only appears in the ancient world after the appearance of the war-chariot, and all-power-fighting evolved [in part]from boxing. To determine if this occurrence is coincidental or causal, one must consider the war-fighting capacity of such a machine. But first let us examine the Homeric military which utilized the war-chariot.

The "armies" of *The Iliad* are in essence nothing more than bands of pirates and bandits that demonstrate a primitive level of group cohesion more reminiscent of modern street gangs than of modern military units. The armies of *The Iliad* are feudal conglomerations headed by chieftains who behave more like gangster rappers fighting over "hip-hop honeys" than captains fighting for strategic and tactical objectives. In this context, the importance of this curious personal vehicle becomes clear.

The chariot only thrives as a weapon in an environment where horses are two small to be ridden individually, and began fading from the battlefield just after the composition of *The Iliad*. A chariot was never an effective shock weapon—and shock** was the element that won ancient battles—because of the poor maneuverability of fixed-axle vehicles, and because the power supply [horses] was entirely vulnerable to enemy weapons due to an exposed position in front of the actual weapons platform. These considerations leave three possible effective uses of the light chariot as an engine of war: as a missile platform, that might be halted a bow-shot from advancing infantry just long enough to loose a volley of arrows before repositioning [the WWII scout jeep with mounted machine gun comes to mind]; as a mobile command post as depicted in the 2004 movie *Troy*, starring Brad Pitt; or as a means of transporting a heavily armored foot-soldier to and from a battle or duel.

This last seems to have been the Homeric use of the chariot. In a war of personal challenges and muscle-powered combat, the ability to show up fresher with heavier gear than your foot-slogging opponent would constitute a significant advantage for the chariot-borne warrior; effectively putting the wealthiest fighters in a class of their own. In this way, such a device for inserting and extracting highly effective fighters into and out of battle, would encourage dueling on a grand scale. In such a martial atmosphere boxing might well become a pastime second only to chariot-racing, for dueling with ancient hand weapons necessitates the ability to circle your opponent [individual behavior at odds with the mechanics of mass battle.] The shorter one's weapons, the more pressing is the need to circle. Just as modern boxers enjoy advantages over modern fencers when the two meet in bouts with ancient weapon systems, ancient boxers most certainly fared better on the dueling ground than in the push and grind of mass battle—and the chariot was a warrior's ticket away from the press of battle to the coveted dueling ground where risks were more tolerably focused and honor amplified.

Not only is there ample evidence indicating that ancient boxing traditions only developed in Mesopotamia, Asia Minor, Crete, Egypt, Greece, India [and possibly China] after the advent of the chariot, in all of the five Western societies listed above, the rise of boxing is contemporary with, or immediately proceeded by, the ascendancy of a chariot-borne warrior-class. Beyond these circumstances—which could be viewed as evidence of a parallel rather than as a causal relationship between chariot-warfare and ritual fist-fighting—are the numerous cultural and religious threads that bind these apparently unrelated arts together.***
    First and foremost is the presence of numerous parallels in the Epic poetry of Greece and

India, most notably between the *Iliad* and the *Ramayana*. The many cultural affinities shared by the ruling classes of India and the Macedonian and Greek invaders led by Alexander included heroic foundation myths preserved in the forms of these epic poems, which tell the tragic tales of doomed chariot-warriors whom not even the gods can save from their mortal fate; the worship of many shared warlike deities; the institution of prize-fighting with fists; and a strong belief in combined-arms doctrine among military field-commanders, which was counter to the tribal nature of most ancient military doctrine. In fact, the notion of combined-arms tactics seems to have arisen with the chariot, which was a brittle high-performance asset requiring integrated support systems to maintain viability on the battlefield.

The Hittites, who relied heavily on chariots and professional infantry, and appear to have been destroyed by the Sea Peoples, decorated the King's Gate of the royal city of Hattusha with a guardian warrior holding an ax and making a fist. Although chariot warriors of the second millennia B.C. were primarily archers, their secondary armament consisted of maces, axes and swords. The use of such short clubbing, chopping and thrusting weapons is echoed in much of the earliest boxing art, which indicates that the overhand hammer-fist was much more respected by these earliest boxers than by fist-fighters of any subsequent period.

The most direct indication of martial influence [military, athletic and equestrian] from

Western Asia or from a common Eurasian
Hinterland is the legend of Pelops [Red-face].
Pelops was a legendary warlord from Asia Minor
for whom the Peloponnese [Red-face-island], the
very cradle of Greek athletics, was named. He is
variously credited with having divine connections,
being a victorious charioteer, founding the first
Olympics, and fathering sons who went on to found
the chief military and athletic centers of the
Peloponnese.

In a very broad and deep sense the ethics of
chariot warfare continued to echo throughout the
civic and military affairs of the greatest empires
through late antiquity. The Etruscan and Roman
practice of riding in a chariot during victory
parades, despite the fact that these people did not
use the chariot as a war engine, is telling. As is the
practice of sacrificing a chariot horse common to
both the Roman Emperors of Italy and the Gupta
Kings of India. The huge social phenomena of
chariot racing in Rome and the later Byzantine
Empire, which remained infused with vicious
politics and blood-thirsty racing tactics well into
the middle-ages, is indicative of the deep-seated
nature of man's obsession with his first true war-
machine.

And finally, the most convincing and all-
encompassing link between the chariot-warriors
who laid the foundations for the ancient world and
the art of ritual fist-fighting, remains the
multifaceted god Apollo. Apollo was the patron of
the Asian Trojans in the *Iliad*, and may correctly be

viewed as symbolizing the legacy of West Asian cultural and martial influences in Greece. Apollo drove the chariot of the sun across the sky by day and through the underworld at night. He was the god of Archery, the weapon of the nomadic charioteer; the god of the bull, the very beast sacrificed for an agon, from the hide of which were made the wrappings for the boxer's fist; the god of boxing who boxed a tax-collecting giant rather than pay a toll; the god of prophecy, traditionally the art of the nomad shaman; the god of music, which accompanied the action of the boxer or all-power-fighter during a bout and the telling of his tale afterward; and the god of plagues, which no doubt ravaged the farming societies who were conquered by the cattle-herding horse-breaking chariot warriors who brought his worship to ancient Hellas.****

The eminence of Apollo as the patron of these many intertwined aspects of suffering and triumph endemic to the life-way of the chariot-warrior did not escape the notice of Homer, and it should not escape ours.

*For a solid academic study of the class and gender politics of Hellenic equestrian and athletic competition see Golden, Mark. *Sport and Society in Ancient Greece*, Cambridge University Press, NY, 1998, pages 1-178

**Herman, Mark & Berg, Richard, *The Great Battles of Alexander: The Macedonian Art of War 338-326 B.C., Deluxe 4th Edition Rules*, GMT Games, LLC, Hanford CA, 2003, pages 5, 24

***Cotterell, Arthur. *Chariot: from Chariot to Tank, the Astounding Rise and Fall of the World's First War Machine*, The Overlook Press, NY, 2004, pages 35-38, 84, 100, 102-04, 105-40, 150-76, 219-98

This is the definitive work in the field, backed by the latest archaeology and executed with rigorous scholarship. Throughout, the author makes clear that the optimal use of the chariot is as a mobile missile platform, which leads him to discount Homer's description of it is a "battle-taxi". However, in numerous instances Cotterell does put fourth evidence that the dominance of the chariot as a mobile archery platform was compromised by aggressive professional infantry before it was eclipsed by the horse-archer and other forms of cavalry.

So, rather than discount Homer's description of chariot tactics as the misunderstanding of a poet, I would prefer to use the Celtic model for chariot tactics as observed by Julius Caesar in 55 B.C. during his invasion of Britain [as a close support vehicle and battle-taxi], and the example of Darius against Alexander at the battles of Issus and Gaugamela [as a command-car]. As Cotterell amply demonstrates throughout his work all of the Western Asian chariot armies except for the

Assyrians [who added a heavy infantryman to their chariot teams] were hard hit by the fast-moving and aggressive infantry fielded by the Sea Peoples who ravaged the Eastern Mediterranean at the time of the Trojan War. These Sea Peoples who brought the empires of the Chariot Lords to their knees were the very same protagonists of Homer's epic, and quite possibly the fathers of Hellenic prize-fighting. Therefore, it is this author's conclusion that the descriptions of chariot use in the *Iliad* represent the attempts of a martial culture based on sea-raiding and hand-to-hand combat to adapt the high-status light-weight chariot to the very mode of warfare that had caused its demise.

**** McNeill, William H. *Plagues and Peoples*, History Book Club, NY, 1976 pages 52, 55, 101, 107, 201, 247, 283

The author discusses the great number of diseases shared by cattle and humans caused from people coming to live in close proximity to these animals during the long process of initial domestication. The various forms of pox, such as cow-pox, chicken-pox and small-pox may be indicated. Small-pox was successfully put to use as a biological weapon by the British military against Native Americans during the war of Pontiac's Rebellion in 18th Century Pennsylvania. Cow-pox was eventually utilized to develop a small-pox vaccine in the 19th Century. The plague of Athens described by Thukydides in *The Peloponnesian War*, is suspected by some historians to have been the disease in question.

Figure 25

A Greek-Style Chariot or *arma* [also *harma*]
From an Etruscan wall painting, Tomba delle Bighe, Tarquinia, c. 500 B.C.

Note the slender well-bred mounts and the small delicate lines of the chariot; no battle car, but a racing vehicle descended from a one-man bronze-age troop transport. Those chariots used to transport a victorious athlete into his hometown may have been of this type.

The Stade

Running as a Martial Art

"—still more Paeonian men the runner [Achilles] would have killed
if the swirling river had not risen, crying out in fury...
..."I am choked with corpses and still you slaughter more"...
..."captain of armies, I am filled with horror!"
And the breakneck runner only paused to answer...
...Down the Trojan front he swept like something superhuman...
...with high hurdling strides, charging against the river...
...they fled as Achilles stormed toward them, shaking his spear..."   "
                    -Homer, *The Iliad, Book 21, Achilles Fights the River*

Achilles was the most important Hellenic martial archetype, more important than Herakles or even Zeus, Thunder-Chief of the gods. It was through the example of warriors such as Achilles, able to gain surprise and position due to their foot-speed and then being able to run-down defeated enemies, that the Greeks gained such a high appreciation for the sport of running. Running appears to have been the basic war-art of the Greeks. As strange as this assertion may seem it makes a lot of martial sense.

The first and most obvious link between running and warfare is the preeminence of the spear in Greek warfare from the earliest to latest of times. As any fighting man knows mobility—footwork if you will—is integral to the timing and power of one's strikes, holds and counters. Historically the bow and the slashing sword and the lance have been employed by horse cultures. Cut & thrust swords and shoulder-fired weapons have generally served as the weapon-of-choice for those warriors who marched to battle. However, the javelin [throwing spear] and the thrusting spear was the preferred weapon of the running warrior— typified by the ancient Greeks, the Slavs of the middle-ages, and the modern Zulus. The mechanics of swordsmanship, archery, axe-wielding and flexible weaponry are not compatible with running, as the runner's stride will ruin his stroke or shot. Also, any swings or cuts delivered by a runner will break his stride. The spear, and its cousins the pike and the javelin may be used effectively at a run, individually, and by massed warriors trained to run in step.

The most feared warrior of myth was Achilles—the unmatched runner.

The only spear-wielding warriors to defeat a modern rifle-armed army were the Zulus, who were greatly feared by their Dutch and English enemies because of their extreme running ability.

The most feared military in Classical and Archaic Greece were the Spartans [*Rope-Makers*] of The Silent Land. But the Spartans most feared by all were the *Skiritai*, a battalion of 600 scouts, renowned for their running ability, recruited from the mountainous region of Arkadia.

The measure of a spear-man's worth is the shock he can deliver to the enemy at the terminus of his charge and the terror his capacity to pursue will instill in the minds of a shaken or ill-prepared foe. Shock and pursuit are military roles which would be completely usurped by the horse-soldiers of late antiquity and the middle ages. But in a world of mountains, islands and small horses, a foot-soldier's foot-speed was paramount and would form the basic exercise of all combat athletes until the days of the Roman Gladiator.

The *stade* [root word for stadium or race-course] or sprint prepared one for the charge, the double-sprint for pursuit, and the long-race for scouting and messenger work. The ancient footrace was no more a game to the ancient warrior than the march is to the modern soldier.

Figure 26.

The Footrace

From a Panathenaic amphora, Bologna, c. 440 B.C.

The runners in the background are running in good form. The runner in the foreground has just received the palm of victory, which he holds in his left hand, and the victor's wreath or crown which he holds in his right hand. The contestants depicted are obviously boys, perhaps five feet tall. The victorious boy has the deep chest of a sprinter, and his build would probably have been common for elite

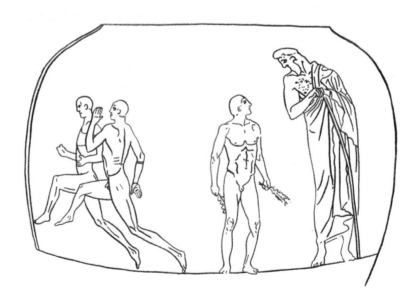

Monomakhia

Hellenik Dueling &The Origins of Greek Boxing

" ...Trojan spearmen
   hurling blows nonstop—a terrible banging
about his temples,
   his [Ajax's] shining helmet clanging under many
blows,
   relentless blows beating his forged cheek irons."
      -Homer, *The Iliad, Book 16: Patroklus
Fights and Dies*

Monomakhia [one-to-one-fighting] was
possibly the longest continuous dueling tradition in
human history. It is a vast subject in its own right
which links more meaningfully with gladiatorial
combat than with unarmed prize-fighting, although
the two are often intertwined. The purpose of this
brief piece is to illustrate the causes and effects that
the practice of monomakhia had on the art of
boxing. All martial cultures possess dueling and

wrestling traditions. Boxing is a much rarer phenomena. Generally boxing emerges from dueling or from dueling and wrestling. The first modern boxing champion, James Figg, was a duelist, wrestler and boxer, and was apparently better at dueling than at the unarmed arts. The passage above might give one a sense for the appeal boxing had to the monomakhaist. Boxing as a preparation for helmet contact is an attractive possibility, since its usefulness has been demonstrated to the author on numerous occassions.* Below are some extracts from *The Iliad* which illustrate uses of the fist in armed combat as well as the oddest boxing match of mythic antiquity. The reader may judge for himself the importance of the fist to the Homeric duelist.

"...overwhelmed by the crushing power of our [godly] fists!...

Achilles had thrust it [his massive shield] forward with his strong fist...

..."But I [Achilles]--whatever fists and feet and strength can do,

that I will do, I swear, not hang back, not one bit...

...I'm off to fight the man, though his fists are fire and his fury burnished iron!"

-Book 20: Olympian Gods in Arms

"Athena's heart jumped, she charged Aphrodite,

overtook her and beat her breasts with clenched fists...

...her [Hera's] left hand seized both wrists of the

goddess [Artemis],
   right hand stripping the bow and quiver off her
shoulders--
   Hera boxed the Huntress' ears with her own
weapons."
       -Book 21: Achilles Fights the River

       In telling the stories of the boxers, ultimate
fighters, pentathletes and wrestlers of antiquity we
will occasionally be drawn into the lethal world of
the duelist, until, with the tide of Christianity and
barbarism that engulfed the pagan world of late
antiquity, that dark art that gave birth to the
unarmed prize-fighter would ultimately return to
reclaim him. By this point in our journey we should
already have a clear understanding that the duel is
both the beginning and the end of boxing, and that
the long-dead subjects of our study understood this
intuitively as well as intellectually.

*From 2001 to 2010 the author engaged in 618
documented full-contact stick fights with fire-
hardened rattan rods for a record of 414 wins, 153
losses and 51 draws. The light hockey helmets used
prevent skull fractures and lacerations but are not
full-proof against concussions—especially those
resulting from rotational strikes to the temple and
ear. It is the author's opinion that his boxing
experience has aided him greatly as a stick-fighter,
particularly when it comes to sustaining combat
after taking head strokes.

Figure 27.

The Hellenik Duel

Scene from the Klazomenae Sarcophagusc. 490 B.C.

Pairs of dueling spearman appear on shields and funeral furnishings more often than on pottery. This particular pair of hoplites are unique in three respects: they fight to the accompaniment of a flute player; they are both using an under-handed grip; and the fighter on the right appears to be wielding a broken spear—although the forward length of the weapon may simply no-longer be visible due to damage to or deterioration of the art work. This is a funerary duel or a phyrric dance celebrating such a duel. In any case it represents the very ritual that laid the foundations for boxing and gladiatorial combat. Fighting with the aspis and spear is extremely tiring and requires great shoulder strength. The round aspis weighed 20 pounds but was designed to permit it to rest on the shoulder, making it practical to use for extended engagements.

The technical aspect most likely cultivated by successful monomakaists was the ability to threaten the head and strike the groin, and conversely to threaten the legs and then strike to the neck. The ability to switch grips from underhand to overhand was important. However, these fighters are probably varying pronated strikes to the high line and supinated strikes to the low line from the same underhanded grip, just as boxers of this period looked to throw the uppercut and the hammerfist from a hyper-pronated high rear-hand position. These spear-fighters demonstrate that boxing principal in reverse. The spring in the knees represents an effort to cover the thighs with the shield and also to keep the legs coiled for a leaping or looping pronated thrust down over the opponent's shield.

Diskus

The Throwing Stone

"But drawing his sharp sword, Achilles charged wildly,
hurtling toward him, loosing a savage cry as Aeneas
lifted a boulder in his hands, a tremendous feat—
no two men could hoist it, weak as men are now,
but on his own he raised it high with ease."
> -Homer, *The Iliad, Book 20: Olympian Gods in Arms*

For the sixth event at the Funeral Games of Patroklus Achilles laid out a single prize, a lump of pig iron. The lump was something of a talisman—a war-prize. It had formerly belonged to Eetion, King of the Kilikians, a famous stone-thrower and father-in-law to Hektor. Eetion was, of course, slain by Achilles, and hence his great iron stone became an Akhaean prize. This iron mass was of great value in the bronze-age, and would also serve as the means—as well as the ends—of contention. The prize was thrown farthest by Polypoetes who surpassed the marks of Epeus, Leonteus and the giant Ajax. Like the other missile weapon arts the diskus throw is treated as a minor event. Battles were won hand-to-hand.

The stone would remain an important weapon in the hands of the slinger and the siege-engineer for many centuries. But the hand-hurled boulder appears to have been a weapon of prehistory that was never important enough to become standard equipment on the bronze-age battlefield. Stone throwing was, however, retained as a martial exercise, with the result that it became a sport, which further resulted in the throwing stone becoming lighter and more aerodynamic. By the 6th Century diskoi were cast of bronze in the characteristic disc shape, measured between six inches and a foot in diameter and weighed from three to fifteen pounds.

Diskoi of the archaic and classical age were sometimes inscribed and dedicated as votive offerings and not intended for competition at all. They also served a political purpose as the signers of a treaty sometimes immortalized their pact on a sacred diskus. Competition diskoi were revered and dedicated to the god or hero of the game. Although the throwing of these rarified stones was a greatly admired art, the activity seems to have become divorced from any notion of war-preparation and to have become a pure expression of physical culture. However, a good throwing arm is not an altogether negligible asset for a boxer, and the hip torque of the classic discus throw may have been useful in the conditioning of wrestlers.

Although it may be beyond our ability to fully appreciate the art of stylized stone-throwing as a preparation for the martial artist, we should not discount the possibility. Sure, the diskus throw may simply have survived as an eccentric game borne on some stone-age battlefield. But, let us not discount the ancients who—though many centuries dead—are the subject of this investigation. The diskus throw really meant something to the ancient Greek sports enthusiast as demonstrated by the fact that it was depicted in art as often as wrestling, boxing and dueling, and more often than any other martial art of the period.

Figure 28.

Phayllos

from an Attic amphora by Euthymides, c. 480 B.C.

Note that Phayllos, though regarded as the consummate finesse athlete of his day, is depicted with powerful hips and thighs. He was the most famous and controversial long-jumper of antiquity, and is said to have heaved a discus 95 feet. The disk being hurled probably weighed between 9 and 15 pounds. A modern Olympic discus weighs 5 pounds. At the time when Phayllos made his throw discoi were evolving from 15 pound stone discs to 9 to 12 pound bronze discs. Phayllos was on the strong side for a pentathlete and appears to have won the pentathlon by winning the jump and discus and then defeating the victor or victors in the run and javelin throw in the wrestling.

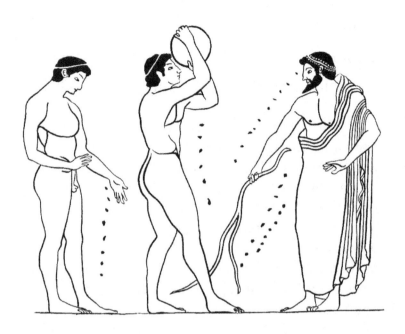

Toxon and Akontion

Bow and Javelin

"Teuker the master archer took up the challenge,
Meriones too...
...They dropped lots in a bronze helmet, and
shook hard
and the cast lot was Teuker's, he would shoot
first..."
　　　　-Homer, *The Iliad, Book 23: Funeral Games
for Patroklus*

Based on the worth of the prizes [10 double
axes to the winner and 10 singles to the loser]
archery was still much respected in Homer's time.
Archery features more in the exploits of heroes
than in athletics [totally abandoned after Homer's
day] because it was a lethal killing art, but not an
art that won major field battles. Battles were won,
and territory taken or protected by breaking the

enemy's will and driving him from the field, not by killing. The respect for the individual prowess of the archer and his value as a mercenary soldier on wilderness campaigns [such as the military quests of Alexander] did not translate into archery being accorded athletic status among the Greeks; because the fathers of the Greek city-states wanted their sons to practice arts that would directly enhance their performance as heavy foot-soldiers in the defense or expansion of their homeland. The Hellenic martial artist was groomed to be a protector not a killer.

The bow and javelin were feared weapons, the bow in particular. Apollo, Herakles, Odysseus and Paris of Troy were all feared archers and boxers of myth. The Kretans, renowned as mercenary archers, were also feared boxers. There does not appear to be any functional link between boxing and archery, but rather a metaphorical one. The boxer is likened to the archer who strikes from afar and dodges to avoid harm, just as the wrestler is equated with the heavily armed fighter of the line. There is some evidence that archery—or at least the flexing of the bow— was practiced as a body-building exercise by wrestlers. Flexing a bow would also provide useful exercise for a boxer seeking to balance his shoulder development to avoid chronic rounding of the shoulders, which is a common affliction among modern boxers, though not evident among the ancients depicted in art.

"Ajax suddenly hurled a glinting spear at

Polydamas,
fast, but the Trojan dodged dark fate himself
with a quick leap to the side—"
            -Homer, *The Iliad, Book 14: Hera Outflanks Zeus*

Spear-throwing retained more relevance to the martial culture of Greece because it was combatable with the thrusting spear and the other gear associated with hoplite warfare. Although the Greek citizen himself would fight as a heavy foot soldier who thrust with his spear, his poorer countrymen, as well as soldiers hired from the high border-lands where hunting was still a common way of life, would provide the majority of the fire-power fielded by Greek armies. The wealthiest soldiers of the classical Greek city-states would ride into battle on horseback, often armed with light spears which they hurled from horse-back. Hence the character of military development did not marginalize the throwing spear, and spear-casting remained an admired martial skill for the entire period under discussion.

Functionally, spear hurling might aid in the development of the muscles employed in the art of punching. However, it is just as likely that the javelin was not an art favored by boxers because of the danger of developing a chronic shoulder condition. The particularly demanding shoulder mechanics of the distance throw favored for sport and mass battle would make it an art avidly avoided by professional-level boxers, who, without the benefits of cortisone injections or rotator-cuff surgery enjoyed by modern athletes, would have to look to prevention as their means of defeating that ever-present specter of the athlete—chronic use-induced injury.

Figure 29.

An Underhanded Dueling Cast

From an Attic kelix, circa 560 B.C.

This is an example of a functional individualized war art. An under-handed cast is a close-range dueling technique that exploits the thrower's shield as a means of concealing the timing and angle of the cast in order to foil the opponent's attempts to dodge, catch or deflect the shaft. For those who doubt the power of such a throw [in this case enhanced with a twisted casting cord] consider that female college softball pitchers throw 59 to 65 miles-per-hour at 43 feet which is equal [when the 17.6 foot range difference is calculated] to a 115 MPH major league baseball throw at 60.6 feet. As with the fencer's thrust, an underhanded throwing technique is also more accurate since the hand stays closer to the body than with an overhand throw. The monomakhaist has raised his lead leg to develop velocity for the cast. As with boxing, the momentum to insure a powerful technique originates at his base in his feet and will be transferred upward through the joints of his body to speed the javelin at maximum velocity. When he stamps down with his lead leg he will have triggered a momentum shift and the throwing spear will fly from his hand, with power

51

and flight stability further enhanced by the added leverage and spinning motion imparted by the casting cord.

*Information on throwing mechanics based on an interview with professional pitching coach Dan Funk on 12/9/04.

Figure 30.
An over-handed athletic cast
From an Attic kelix, circa 525 B.C.

A highly evolved stylistic sport based on the casting techniques employed in mass battle. Casts for mass battle would be predominantly overhand but not for reasons of power or accuracy. An overhand cast was important in mass battle because it permitted casting from horse back; casting over the heads of companions in forward ranks; and more easily achieved a controlled angle of descent beyond an enemy shield-wall and forward troops into the exposed neck, collar and chest of reserve troops than did an underhanded cast. Again, the example of javelin throwing points out the importance of all Greek athletics as indirect methods for preparing citizen-soldiers for the crisis of mass battle. Athletic casts appear to have been rated for distance so long as they stayed within the boundary of the casting area, while equestrian casts were rated for accuracy.

Pentathlon

The Five Exercises

"...they are well adapted both for bodily exertion and foot-speed. In the prime of life, beauty lies in being naturally adapted for the toils of war... one who excels in both boxing and wrestling is fit for the pankration. But he who excels in everything is fit for the pentathlon."
    -Aristotle, *Rhetoric*, c. 360 B.C.

In the passage above the most prolific philosopher of ancient Greece points out that the pentathlete was considered to be a combat-athlete. It might also do well to add that Aristotle would most certainly consider modern American football a combat sport. The ancients had a much deeper and broader definition of martial arts than do modern people, because of their deeper intellectual, cultural, and practical relationship with warfare and those vestigial war arts that moderns think of as sports.

Pentathletes appear to have been drawn from the upper-class, based on the number of general officers among pentathletes—which exceeds the number of generals drawn from all other classes of athlete combined. As a sport that required excellence in at least three disciplines—at least one of which had little similarity to the other two necessary for victory—the pentathlete would require more training time than other more specialized athletes. Proficiency in two arts and excellence in three requires a broad band of physical ability and mental adaptability; which, if nothing else, helped to determine which men of the leadership class possessed the qualities necessary for the leadership --and the combat demands of such small-scale leadership roles—of citizen militia force. There is much controversy among modern scholars as to how the winner of the pentathlon was determined. Having reviewed the various arguments and the latest archaeological evidence from a combat arts perspective this author can offer the following highly probable sequence of events.

The Five Exercises

Exercise 1: stone-throwing

The players drew lots for the order of the throw and then each threw the diskos once, the distances being marked with pegs, and then the cycle was repeated three times at Olympia and five at Rhodes.

Exercise 2: jumping

Each athlete jumped in order according to the distance of their throws. A jump probably consisted of three consecutive standing long jumps, aided by the swinging of the weights. The longest ancients jumps credited were Phayllos at 50 feet injuring his leg in the process [478 B.C.], and a jump of 33 feet by Khionis of Sparta [664 B.C.]

Exercise 3: javelin-throw

The athletes probably cast their javelins in three to five turns --probably based on the order of their jumping distances. A throwing lane—perhaps the running track—was designated. Casts landing outside of the lane would be discounted.

Victory would be granted to an athlete who swept these three events.

Exercise 4: running

If there was no sweep of the unique events a foot race of one or two lengths of the track would be run.

Victory would now be granted to an athlete who had won three of the four events.

Exercise 5: wrestling

If no athlete had won three of the first four

events, than those athletes with victories would wrestle. If there were three or four victors then lots would be drawn. The pentathlon may often have come down to a wrestling match between the winner of the two throwing events and the winner of the two track events—obviously a bout of great interest between two variant body types. A showdown between four winners would net three bouts, and a wrestling trial to sort out the best of three victors would feature two bouts with one wrestler drawing a bye.

If no athlete prevailed in three of the five events then the prize would be dedicated to the patron god of the games. This practice may possibly account for the small roster of known pentathlon victors compared to other events as well as the votive discoi dedicated at various athletic centers.

Figure 31.

Progress of the Pentathlete

From a PanAtheniac amphora, circa 525 B.C.

This illustration depicts the events unique to the pentathlon as engaged in by a single athlete, or by a group of idealized athletes. From left to right:

31.1. Swinging the jumping weights to gain momentum [looks to be an excellent exercise for the important punching muscles of the abdomen and latismis dorsi]

31.2. Gaining momentum for the akontion cast [good torso work for developing a fighter's body]

31.3. Preparing to initiate the twisting action unique to the distance through [good for developing the muscles that expand and protect the rib cage]

31.4. The initial phase of hurling the akontion that would immediately proceed the mechanics depicted in figure 31.2

The Lives of the Pentathletes

720 B.C. Homer's Odyssey details the exercises of the pentathlon as important but separate.

708 B.C. The pentathlon becomes an Olympic event.

664 B.C. Khionis [?] of Sparta wins the foot race at the 29th Olympiad, but failed to win the pentathlon even though he jumped 33 feet.

628 B.C. The first pentathlon for boys at the 38th Olympiad is won by Eutelidas [?] of Sparta, who then went on to win the wrestling. The Eleans— possibly in reaction to Eutelidas' accomplishment— ban the boys' pentathlon.

550 B.C. Kratios [*Strongest*] of Athens wins the pentathlon at the PanAthenae

524 B.C. Running in armor is instituted at the 64th Olympiad, and is won by Damaratus.

c.500 B.C. Aenetus of Amyklae died [probably of heatstroke] as he was being crowned victor for the Olympic pentathlon. Theopompus [*Priest-Conducting*] of Heraea won the Olympic pentathlon. Damiskus [*Subduing-?*] of Messene [probably in Sicily] wins the boy's Olympic pentathlon and took the mens' prize at Nemea and the Isthmus. Tisamenos [*Great-Spirit*] of Elis hears a prophecy that he would win five amazing contests. So he trains for the pentathlon and enters the Olympics.

Heironymos [*Sacred-?*] of Andros wins the diskos
throw. Next Tisamenos wins the jump. Heironymos
then wins the javelin throw. Tisamenos comes back
to win the foot-race. With two victories each the
men wrestle for the prize and Heironymos is
victorious. Tisamenos, being the son of a prophet,
would not accept that the prophecy had been
wrong, so he enlisted with the Spartan army as an
adviser, and they won all five battles that he
advised them to fight. If Tisamenos were a man of
the 21st Century he would be a book-maker in Las
Vegas. Backing 5th Century Sparta on the battlefield
was like betting on the German Army in 1940 or
Mike Tyson in the 1980s. Eurybates [*Broad-Step*] of
Argos wins the Nemean pentathlon and
distinguished himself in battle.

    c.490 B.C.Timokreon [*Esteemed-Butcher*] of
Rhodes is an undistinguished pentathlete who is
ostracized by his fellow Rhodians. During his exhile
he was patronized by another exhile by the name of
Themistokles, who was a inn-keeper, thief, loan-
shark and hitman, who eventually committs suicide.
Timokreon apparently worked as a butcher at
Themistokles' inn, and spent some time as a
drinking companion, informer, and entertainer
among the fabulously rich Persian elite. Invited to
the court of the Persian King [probably Darius I] for
a feast, Timokreon impresses the King of Kings by
eating and drinking more than anyone thought
possible. The day after the feast Timokreon fights
seven boxing exhibitions against Persian fighters,
scoring seven KOs. He then begins shadow-boxing.

When the King asks why he is doing this, Timokreon responds, "Because I still have an equal number of knock-out punches for anyone willing to face me." After his death Timokreon is immortalized in the following epitaph, composed by the famous Persian-hating poet, Simonides of Kos...

"Having eaten much, drunk much, and speaking

Insults of many men, here lies

Esteemed-Butcher of Rhodes."

Diophon [*Heavenly-Blood*] is immortalized by Simonides for winning the Isthmian and Pythian pentathlon.

482 B.C. Phaylos [*Commoner*] of Kroton wins the pentathlon at Delphi

480 B.C. Phaylos captained a ship manned by his fellow Krotonian athletes and helps defeat the Persian armada at the Battle of Salamis. Ikkus of Tarentum—famous for his austere training—wins the pentathlon at the 75th Olympiad.

478 B.C. Phaylos wins the foot race at Delphi and goes on to compete in the pentathlon: casting the diskos the farthest, and then making his famous 50 foot jump, tearing a leg muscle in the process. Unable to hurl the javelin or run the foot-race, Phaylos goes on to victory by prevailing in wrestling.

476 B.C. An athlete of Taras [Tarentum] won the pentathlon at the 76th Olympiad.

472 B.C ...amos of Miletus won the pentathlon at

the 77th Olympiad.

468 B.C. ...tion of Taras [Tarentum] won the pentathlon at the 78th Olympiad.

450 B.C. Automedes [*Free-Persian*] of Phleius won the pentathlon at Nemea.

467 B.C. The destruction of Tyrins by Argos.

The boys' pentathlon was introduced at the 53rd Nemead and won by Sogenes [*?-Born*] of Aegina.

c.450 B.C. The sons of Kleinus of Argos became famous by sweeping the following events at Nemea and the Isthmus: Kreathus [?] in the pentathlon; Timodermus [Honored-?] in running; Kres [*The Body*] in wrestling; and Diokles *[Heavenly-Key]* in boxing. Herodikus of Slymbria began the practice of therapeutic exercise after curing himself through athletics.

400s B.C. The following Elean pentathletes win victories on uncertain 4th to 3rd Century dates: Anaukhidas, 1 Olympiad; Aeskhines[?] 2 Olympiads; Eupolemus [*Good-at-War*] 2 Pythiads & 1 Nemean; Pythokles [?]1 Olympiad; Klienomakhus [*?-Fighter*] 1 Olympiad; Klearetus [?] 1 Olympiad; Theodorus [*priest-?*] 1 Olympiad; Menakles [*Abiding-Repute*] 1 Olympiad

c.400 B.C. Alexibius [*Protector-of-Life*] of Heraea wins the pentathlon at an Olympiad of uncertain date. Lykus [*Wolf*] of Messene [probably in Sicily] wins the pentathlon at an Olympiad of uncertain date.

390 B.C. Krates [*Taker*] of Athens wins the

pentathlon at the PanAthenae

383 B.C. Stomius [*Foremost,* or *Point,* or *Edge*] of Elis wins the Nemean pentathlon.

381 B.C. Stomius wins Nemean pentathlon.

380 B.C. Stomius wins the pentathlon at the 100th Olympiad.

379 B.C. Stomius wins the pentathlon at Nemea.

376 B.C. Antiokhus [?] of Lepreus wins the pentathlon at 101st Olympiad.

375 B.C. Antiokhus wins the Nemean pentathlon.

373 B.C. Antiokhus wins the Nemean pentathlon.

372 B.C. Antiokhus wins the pentathlon at the 102nd Olympiad, and goes on to win the pankration!

371 B.C. Antiokhus serves as the Arkadian ambassador to the Persian King.

Stomius leads the Elean cavalry into battle and slays the enemy general in single combat.

369 B.C. Hymson of Elis, who had suffered a muscular disease as a boy, and had rehabilitated himself through athletics wins the Nemean pentathlon.

368 B.C. Hymson wins the pentathlon at the 103rd Olympiad.

350 B.C. Xenokles [?] of Athens wins the boy's pentathlon at the PanAthenae.

332 B.C. Kallippos [*Beautiful-Horse*] was fined for bribing his opponents at Olympia

Olympia and Olympus

The Grove of the High-gods: A Warrior's View of the 1st Olympiad, 776 B.C.

"Words no more—he sprinted toward Troy,
heart pounding for some mighty act, rushing on
like an unbeaten stallion drawing a speeding
chariot,
sweeping across the plain in easy, tearing strides—
so Achilles ran on, driving legs and knees."
> -Homer, *The Iliad*, from *The Death of Hektor*

Rank-breaker, war-chief of Rope, was the most feared warrior of The Silent Land. A man little given to pilgrimages and impatient with deal-makers, he had journeyed to the Grove of the High Gods for this truce-contest with some reservations. Though now, after greeting his rivals and allies and even some proud strangers, at the head of his picked fighters, he was pleased to have come.

The grove was at the foot of the hill where the guides said that the Thunder-chief had thrown down the Titan-chief. The tour of the grove reminded Rank-breaker and his men that they were the descendents of conquerors, and that they had war-brothers in other lands. The Temple of the Sky-mother, the great altar of the Thunder-chief and the Earth-shaker, the five altars of the young-warriors, and even the pillar of Wine-drinker and the tomb of Red-face, lent a sense of power to this gathering.

Despite all of the deal-making and cross-talking of the kings who had arranged this truce, and the fanciful stories about Red-face, Ox-eater, and the other conquerors told by the self-important little guides, every war-chief knew himself to be here for two reasons: to measure himself and his men against the best war-fighters of Red-face Island, and to seize the crown of agony by running like Achilles, and proving according to the oldest tradition his right to lead, by leaving the others behind in the dust of defeat.

Although Rank-breaker was a good charge-and-turn fighter, he was more of a clinch-and-gut-stab man; and had no illusions that he was going to be able to outrun all of these lanky Elean cow-herds and scrawny Arkadian shepherds. However, whatever their disadvantages, Rank-breaker was confident that he and his men would please the Thunder-chief and the other war-gods. He had some hard-running scouts amongst his shield-men—and they had hiked here from beyond the mountains, unlike those boat-hugging tender-foots coming up from the riverbank. Besides, somebody had already scratched out a wrestling pit, and if he knew his boys they'd break a few legs before race-day.

Olympic Origins

The Episodic Evolution of the Ancient Olympiad

"Endymion set his [three] sons to run a race at Olympia for the throne; Epeion won, and was awarded the kingdom, and his subjects were, from then on, named Epeans.
 -Pausanias, *Description of Greece*

This reconstruction of the origins of the Olympic agon is based on the historical records of the Eleans as related by Pausanias and the modern archaeological record. All dates are approximate and are B.C.

1700: Olympia is a center for the worship of Gaea, Rhea and Kronos [*Saturn*] by the pre-Greek inhabitants. The area appears to have been sacred to the maternal agricultural society that was being displaced from the east and north by the paternal cattle-based culture of the Indo-European Greeks.

The antiquaries of Elis referred to the pre-Greek inhabitants as the Golden Race, and claimed that they had raised a temple at Olympia in honor of Kronos, king of heaven, consort of the Earth Mother.

c.1500: The daktyls [*fingers*] or kouretes [*Young-warriors*] of Mt. Ida on Krete, establish a mission at Olympia. The leader of these five chiefs—reportedly brothers—was Herakles [*Hera's-honor*], who introduced the worship of Zeus and Hera and the olive tree, and established the Olympic agon as a competition for his younger brothers. The intervals between each agon were 4 years, 1 year for each of Herakles' brothers. It is likely that the daktyls were conquerors rather than missionaries, as the folk legends of the Olympic origins speak of Zeus defeating Kronos in wrestling for the throne of Olympia and then holding games in honor of his victory. In these games Apollo, god of excellence, defeats Ares, god of war, in boxing and Hermes, messenger of the gods, in running. These myths of the domination and excellence; of the Earth Mother's consort being defeated by the bull-eating Thunder-chief, and of Apollo winning out over the naturally gifted Ares and Hermes, reflect the will-to-power of a warrior society justifying the oppression of a conquered people. In this respect the Olympian gods served the early Greek conquerors in much the same fashion as Christianity did the conquistadors in New Spain and the puritans in New England.

1470: The eruption of Thera [possibly known as the flood of Deukalion to the ancient Greeks] strikes the death blow to Classical Minoan civilization, and Greek pirate chiefs expand their activities, including the promotion of the cult of Zeus, who is appeased by offerings of cattle and through agonistic rites.

1420: Klymenus, a descendent of Herakles, conquers Olympia, raises an Altar in honor of Herakles, and reestablishes the Olympic agon.

1400: Endymion defeats Klymenus and established an agon to determine which of his sons will rule.

1370: The last Minoan center, Knossos, is destroyed by Greek raiders. Pelops [*Red-face*] of Lydia immigrates to Pisa and wins the throne in a chariot race with King Oenomaus. He takes the border region of Olympia from Epeius, conducts the Olympiad in honor of Zeus, and builds a temple to Hermes. The entire body of land would eventually be named the Peloponnese [*Red-face-island*]. Eleius, grandson of Endymion, seizes the kingdom of Epeius, and thereafter the country is named Elis.

1300: Amythaon of Elis wins control of Olympia from the descendents of Pelops. He and his descendents Pelias, Neleus, and Augeas continue the ancient practice of holding Olympiads, according to 4 year cycles, or as events inaugurating the new king's rule. Zeus, Hera and Herakles are worshipped.

1200: In the wake of the Trojan War the brutal war-chief Herakles of Thebes conquers Olympia, and holds an agon to celebrate his triumph. He is credited with winning the wrestling and the all-power-thing, while Kastor wins the foot-race and Polydeukes the boxing match.

1100: The Aetolian mercenary Oxylus conquers Elis, and is the last king of the heroic age to hold an Olympiad. The Temple of Hera is raised at Olympia. The invasion of the Dorian Greeks begin.

776: King Iphitus of Elis, a descendent of Oxylus, is advised by the Delphik Oracle to re-institute the Olympic agon in the interest of peace. Iphitus and King Kleosthenes [*Lion-strong*] of Pisa make an Olympic treaty. Agons are held sporadically at Olympia, which is the center of a disputed border region. The first Olympiad of "the unbroken tradition" is held, and the name of a victor in the foot-race is recorded. The name of King Lykurgus of Sparta is entered on the sacred treaty discus, possibly at a later date.

708: The first recorded victors in combat events are Lampis the pentathlete and Eurybatus the wrestler, both Spartans. This event establishes the ethic of combat sports for military preparedness, and inaugurates over a century of Spartan athletic dominance. The Olympic agon soon becomes the single most important event in Greece, as leading men gather every 4 years to compete in the rituals of martial excellence.

The Big Twelve

The Nature and Foundations of Greek Religion

"...truly a sacred place, the home built for a god when the world was young and men had not yet forgotten that when the gods are mocked they punish us by leaving us."
                    -Gene Wolfe, *Soldier of the Mist*

The religious life of Archaic Greece was largely a matter of acts committed amongst the thousands of temples and shrines that cluttered the broken landscape like so many windows into the unseen, where the legend-shrouded past, the mysteries of the present, and the looming future might be addressed by man. As powerfully concise as their vocabulary was, the ancient Hellenes had no single word to describe the religious experience. This realm of ancient life was different in scope and purpose than the modern experience—being both more and less.

The word *therapeia* [service] covers the holy aspect of life, which consisted of the maintenance of god-houses, spirit-shrines and hero-tombs; sacrifice [burnt for the gods and sometimes poured out on the earth to appease the dead and the earth-spirits]; agonistic rites, and feasts. Such was the civic side of the religious equation, which we might liken to ethics. The mysterious—and often dark side—of spiritual life was embodied in the word *deisidaimonia* [fear-of-spirits]. This aspect of religion reflected its origin, as a method for mediating between man and the apparently irrational, vague and awesome manifestations of a natural world that was not yet understood on a scientific basis.

The fear of spirits and the desire to be favored by the unseen powers were expressed by the maintenance of a sacred space [more like a supernatural executive suite than a place of worship] for the god; purification of one's self from guilt by ritual washing, removal of materials relating to an offense [such as a murder weapon] and even the ostracism of a person designated as a scapegoat for an entire community; and also the appeasement of supernatural forces through sacrifice and agonistic rites.

Within this multifaceted context the multitude of minor gods and earth-spirits, as well as heroes both cursed and revered, were conceived of as being ruled over by six male and six female super-deities who embodied the qualities later aggregated to the one God of Christianity. However, underpinning this entire perception of human-like deities was the idea that even they were bound to the powerful tides of Fate, just as humanity was bound to the mortal world. A sense of tragedy permeated the sacred on every level.

The twelve Olympian gods were in some cases composite deities reflecting a centuries-long process of invasion, conquest and assimilation. The equal number of male and female gods reflects untold shifts in the spiritual paradigm and centuries of cultural upheaval and compromise. The dominance of the invading indo-Europeans is indicated by the preeminence of Zeus, the sky god, and the fact that he and his 11 chief gods were said to live atop Mount Olympus.

The Olympian pantheon was conceived of as a supernatural clan [Various leagues of comic-book superheroes come to mind.] ruled by Zeus. His many cult titles suggest that he usurped the functions of many minor gods. He was the supreme god, and, in many ways, the later God of Christianity seems to be a composite of Zeus and Fate, just as the earth-gods and earth-spirits are later represented by Satan and his minions, and the numerous minor gods are replaced by the litany of Catholic saints.

The heavenly tribe ruled by the god of thunder consisted of Hera [his jealous wife], guardian of marriage; Poseidon, spiteful ruler of the sea, breaker of horses [an earlier nomad sky-god];

Aphrodite, goddess of sea-foam and semen;
Artemis, goddess of the wild; Athene, goddess of
thought, skill and war; Demeter, the Earth Mother;
Apollo, schizophrenic boy-wonder, god of the sun,
pestilence and healing, boxing and higher thought;
Hermes, guide of travelers, athletes, and the dead;
Hephaestus, a fire-spirit of the Near East who
appears to have been promoted to a military arms
contractor by Zeus, and was to Homer's Achilles
what Q was to Ian Flemming's James Bond; Ares,
brutal god of war hailing from the barbarian North;
and Hestia, goddess of the home, who was
eventually displaced by Dionysus, patron of sex,
drugs and drinking songs.

Further reading:
--Finley, M. I. *The World of Odysseus*, The Folio
Society, London, 2002, pages 2-4, 8-12, 41
--Parrinder, Geoffrey. *World Religions: From Ancient
History to the Present*, NY, 1971, pages 146-58
--Harrison, Jane Ellen. *Prolegomena to the Study of
Greek Religion*, as reprinted in *The World Treasury
of Modern Religious Thought*, edited by Jaroslav
Pelikan, Little Brown, London, 1990

The Curses of Moline & Lysippe

Tribalism and a Mother's Wrath

There are three stories concerning the practice of Eleans [whose home-town of Elis officiated the Olympic agon] not competing at the Isthmian agon, officiated by the Korinthians. The tale most believed by Pausanias was that the murder of the sons of Aktor [Siamese twins who were an unbeatable chariot racing team—think about it!] by Herakles resulted in their mother, Moline, imposing a curse on any Elean who dared to compete in the Isthmian agon; the stated reason being that the Korinthians refused to bar the Argives from the agon for not giving up Herakles to the Eleans.

The least likely tale of the Elean boycott of the Isthmian agon supposedly stemmed from an offering of a golden image made by Kypselus, tyrant of Korinth, at Olympia. According to this story,

Kypselus died before having his name engraved on the offering, and the Eleans refused the requests of his successors that his name be engraved on the golden image that he had dedicated to Zeus. This tale was contradicted by Korinthian participation at Olympia, and the gift of the Chest of Kypselus [see Figure 36 in *The Gods of Boxing*].

The tale that this author finds to ring most true is the following...

The boy athletes Lampus and Philanthus of Elis, sons of the leading Elean Prolaus, and his wife Lysippe, journeyed to Korinth to compete in the Isthmian agon. Both boys entered for the pankration, and one of them intended to wrestle as well. At some point between their swearing-in and the call to wrestle, they were strangled and choked to death by their opponents. [This indicates a period of segregating the athletes in a holding area or preparatory facility between the registration or oath-taking and the actual contest, echoed by the "house" aspect of the reality show *The Ultimate Fighter*.] This event caused Lyssipe to declare a curse on any Elean who would participate in the agon overseen by the officials who had permitted the murder of her sons.

Since the panHellenic agons themselves were in fact truces, and had their origins in the celebration of conquests, the forging of alliance, and the making of peace, such a curse by a mother of Elis resulting from the failure of Korinth to bring the murderers of her sons to justice would be reasonable. It is the author's opinion that an ancient tribal curse had been long-standing at the time of the murder of the sons of Lyssipe, and that she invoked the ancient tradition of Moline in honor of her wronged sons.

Timon of Elis, war hero of the Hellenistic Age, refused to compete at the Isthmus after sweeping the other three panHellenic agons. For this the Eleans honored him with the following inscription on the base of his statue in the Altis:

"Sisyphus' land [Korinth] he did not visit for the quarrel

Over the murder of the Molionids."

This author was unable to determine if Timon lived before or after Lysippe.

Deities Sacred to Greek Fighters

Notes: Female deities are in italic.

*Denotes a hero—a deified person who may have lived between 1700-800 B.C.

**Denotes a deified person who is known to have lived in historic times.

***Deity of late antiquity.

In ancient Greece any time prior to 750 B.C. may be regarded as "pre-historic" times, in that written accounts of events are not recorded for this period, leaving the historian entirely dependent upon archeological evidence and inferences from surviving oral traditions. The deities are listed according to their apparent order-of-importance to ancient fighting men & women as varied as bullfighters & professional soldiers.

The god's Hellenic name is followed by the Roman and then by its spiritual province.

Zeus, Jupiter [Jove]: Kingship, athletics, oaths, laws, rules, wrestling, marriage, home, hospitality, property, salvation, lightning, thunder, fertility, justice, victory-giver, Olympic and Nemean agons

Herakles*   Hercules: labors [such as a siege], pankration, monomakhia,wrestling, hunting, victory, business, boxing, strength

Apollo: artistry, music, excellence-in-victory, boxing, archery, prophecy, healing, wolves, success, creativity, Pythian agons

Ares, Mars: war, vengeance, storms & hurricanes

Hermes, Mercury   travel, contests, running, wrestling, magic, alchemy

Serapis***: travel, healing, traveling athletes of Alexandria

Poseidon, Neptune: oceans, earthquakes, Isthmian agons

Dioskuri*, Dioscuri: "the manly twins of Zeus" Kastor & Polydeukes, worshipped together for luck in war or other perilous undertaking

Kastor, Castor: monomakhia

Polydeukes, Pollux boxing

Nike: victory

Astarte: war, vengeance, victory, fire, sexual prowess

Athena: war, strength, battle, war-victory, Athens, panAthenian agons

Enyo, Bellona: war

Asklepios,* Aesculapius: healing, medicine

Palaistra, Palaestra: wrestling

Pelops*: Olympia, Olympics, chariot racing, the southern peninsula of Greece or Peloponnese

Akhilles*, Achilles: war, monomakhia, running

Hektor*, Hector: bravery, honor [a Roman favorite]

Aeneas*: virtues of a warrior [a Roman favorite]

Odysseus*, Ulysses: cunning, ruthlessness

Ajax*: strength-in-battle

Kronos , Saturn: agriculture, happiness restrained by misfortune, bodily disorders, gloom & lead [lead-poisoning?], time, age

Atlas: strength

Pythia: serpents, Pythian agons

Paeon: physician of the gods

Hera, Juno: women, female athletes

Theogenes**: healing, prosperity

Theseus*: Attika, Athens, beast-fighting, wrestling, boxing

Koronis: medicine

Artemis, Diana: hunting, the moon

Hades, Pluto: death

Boreas: The North Wind, much respected by sailors

Alkmene: midwinter, mother of Herakles

Thetis: mother of Akhilles

Proteus: the sea

Alkyone: the sea

Amphitrite: the sea

Doris: the sea

All-Power-Fighting

Alphito: barley flour, destiny, the moon

Hipposthenes: Wrestling, strength, Spartan warriors

Note: Praying for a victory at sea must have been as complicated as the actual fight!

Struggle of Hands

Wrestling from Odysseus to Khilon, 1220 to 323 B.C.

"The champions [Ajax and Odysseus], belted tight, stepped onto the dug-up
and clinched each-other hard with big brawny arms,
locked like rafters a master builder joins together,
slanting into a tarred roof to fight the ripping winds.
And their backbones creaked as wrestling hands sought submission-holds and sweat ran down their spines
and clusters of raw welts rose on ribs and shoulder slippery, bloody red, and still they grappled, harder..."

-Homer, *The Iliad, Book 23: Funeral Games for Patroklus*

All-Power-Fighting

The quote above is a vivid and accurate picture of the type of stand-up wrestling which evolved into boxing among the Indo-European chariot peoples—and, by Homer's day, some 2750 years ago, the spectators who had gathered to see a "fight" were already yawning...,"A stalemate. And the troops were growing bored." This factor, the disapproval of a bored audience, was already infecting wrestling in its infancy. The poet goes on to describe how Ajax talked the smaller but more skilled Odysseus into "working" the bout. But Odysseus tricked the giant by allowing himself to be hoisted, but then hooking Ajax's leg behind the knee—while the big guy attempted some sort of supplex—so that he fell across the giant's chest and pinned him to the ground. They went down again in a tangle, and then rose for a third throw, but Achilles called off the bout to avoid injury to either of his two captains.

If Odysseus and Ajax failed to entertain their own men, who were no doubt knowledgeable wrestlers themselves, it is no wonder that wrestling latter lost its spectator appeal among the mobs of Imperial Rome and the carnival crowds of 1930s America. While wrestling was the foundation art of Hellenic boxing and pankration, and one of the three pillars of mass battle preparation [the others being boxing and running] it failed to entertain on the level of boxing. Therefore, of the three unarmed Hellenic combat sports, wrestling would remain the least popular though most practiced.

The appeal of wrestling as a war-fighting preparation for part-time spearmen who trained to fight in close order, is analogous to its appeal to the pankratiast [all-power-fighter] who trained to wage his own naked, miniature, total war. The primary value of up-right grappling to the warrior was to develop a powerful and adaptive base. The ability to stay on one's feet in the surging crush of battle when thousands of athletic bodies hurtled together was a life-saving device. Any man who went down under this tide of armored spearmen would either be crushed by the tread of his comrades, or speared by the butt spikes of the advancing enemy. To even be regarded as a warrior meant keeping your feet. The lesson of the modern ultimate-fighter is most telling...

When cage combat first hit pay-per-view television in the early 1990s ground-grapplers ruled. As boxers and wrestlers waged war through the 1990s and into the first decade of the 21st Century it became apparent that the boxer or kick-boxer could not strike effectively without a strong grappling base.

A key figure in the evolution of this sport was Randy Couture, a former Olympic gold medalist in Greco-Roman wrestling, who once out-boxed a world-class kick-boxer, Chuck Liddell, from the security of his upright grappling base. In modern MMA wrestling ability is a pre-requisite for the application of boxing ability. On the ancient battlefield it was no different. The ability to stay on one's feet was a prerequisite for the application of weaponry.

Author's note on mass battle: In 1978, during a stampede outside of a rock concert in Pittsburgh Pennsylvania, I was caught in the middle of a mass of approximately 10,000 people. I was barely able to keep my toes on the ground as the crowd swayed and surged. My friend, a heavyweight wrestler, and another man about his size, decided to plow through the crowd, while others—such as myself—teetered in their wake. After that day it has never been hard for me to imagine how much of an asset a powerful man with his strength centered about his hips would have been in the crush of a mass battle. It is no wonder that the Spartan kings chose Olympic victors as their battle companions.

What follows is not a comprehensive study of ancient wrestling techniques. Rather it consists of two samples of the basic initial posture. However, the chronological study of the lives of the ancient wrestlers is a comprehensive one.

After the period under discussion wrestling continued as a second tier Olympic event and as a very important aspect of all-power-fighting, which, by 212 B.C. had eclipsed boxing as the supreme test of athleticism at Olympia.

A Fighter's View

The Contests at Dolphins

A Wrestler's View of the 12th Pythiad, 530 B.C.

"What god drove them to fight with such fury?"
-Homer, *The Iliad*, from *The Rage of Achilles*

The First Draw

The lots for the first round of the hand-struggle had been drawn. The field was a strong one but narrow. After Sheep's last performance had resulted in so many injuries to the other Hellenes only the best hands had drawn lots for this celebration of the Archer's victory over the Snake. At this first drawing there were only six: his rival the Bull-eater; a towering Argive stone-heaver; a vicious Spartan front-line-fighter; the Athenian all-power-fighter who had awed the on-lookers at the last Olympiad; an impossibly fat barbarian that some rich Priestess from Land-bridge-town had gotten past the Oracle; and that pesky little runner

from back home who had won the five-exercises...
As the pairings were revealed father hovered
behind his shoulders, whispering his predictions
for each bout. Finally, when it was announced that
he would be paired with the Argive, father hissed,
"Good draw Sheep. He's the strongest—and tall—
break his ribs and the rest will be too rattled to get
their asses low in the clinch."

The Argive's brother stepped forward and
withdrew him from the contest. No explanation was
given or expected. The Argive would suffer the
simple nameless fate of the unknown.

The runner had drawn a bye. He and Sheep
sat out while the Spartan was tossed by the Bull-
eater, and the Athenian dropped the barbarian on
his shoulder, breaking the collarbone.

The Second Draw

Sheep drew a match with the runner. Father,
said, and loudly enough for the runner's uncle to
here, "If that little goat runs you around forget
about the throw. Just step on his feet and break his
ankles."

The runner was withdrawn by his oldest
brother, who claimed kinship with their fellow
townsmen.

The bout between the Bull-eater and the
Athenian was the event of the day. The boxers were
kept waiting for two full measures of the sun while
the bull-eater struggled for three clean throws
against the wily Athenian; who couldn't get a throw
on the big man, though he rolled with him in the

dust eight times. The all-power-fighters watched the hand-struggle with great interest, looking for any weakness that might show in the Athenian's clinch work. The Bull-eater finally settled for an ugly belly throw. Father petitioned the sacral-judges to rule it a foul fall. But they gave it to the big man.

The Third Draw

Sheep and the Bull-eater symbolically drew the only two lots from the Archer's helmet. The Bull-eater, who trained himself, walked over to sheep and handed over his lot with a heavy sigh. They had struggled often, and Sheep had always won. As fatigued as the mountain-shepherd was, the struggle would have been pointless. Father slapped him on the back, and said, "A no-duster. We'll take it."

The elder sacral-judge retrieved the lots, which would be dedicated to the Archer, and placed the sacred bay-leaf crown on his head. He was getting old enough to start making some of his own decisions. He would speak to the Athenian about training at his wrestling-ground for the upcoming Nemean contest. If the Argive declined to grapple him there, then he would dog him to Hera's Shield Contest and petition the High Priestess herself for the right to contest for the shield at Argos. He would goad the stone-thrower onto the dug-up and make father proud.

The Gods of Wrestling

1220 to 720 B.C.

"The Argives used the aulos [double-flute] at the
wrestling contest they called the Stheneia
[Strength-gathering]."
-Plutarch

The origins of boxing and wrestling were
deeply intertwined. In late antiquity, Plutarch and
other scholars were convinced of this connection,
as they cited the statements handed down from
legendary figures from classical antiquity. It was
said that the great Argive musician Auletes Sakadas,
who had won three Pythian victories for his flute-
play, claimed that Polyduekes, the patron god of
boxing, had invented the aulos. The aulos also
provided the music for the sacrifice of sacred
animals, as well as for the jump of the pentathletes.
The recognition of rhythmic concepts in relation to
combat was an ancient insight that is not always
shared by modern martial artists. Wrestling also

shared divine blessings. And it is on those primal sacred grounds, that the great antiquity of wrestling may be determined. In search of insight into the connections of wrestling with boxing and music the author interviewed coach Dan Funk, a veteran of over 500 scholastic wrestling matches and 25 amateur boxing bouts.

"Wrestling is a tantric event. Wrestling is more about action and emotion than boxing. Boxing was always more analytical for me because of my [poor] sight. In wrestling you're always connected to this other organism. I didn't see. I felt. It happened. Everything was felt, it was very musical—every wrestler has a song in his head. I don't have any visual memories of any of my wrestling matches— my boxing bouts left a more visual impact, and I think it was the same for the crowd. If I was wrestling a fish I could play to the audience. But with another guy at my skill level it had to be boring for the uninitiated spectator."
-Dan Funk, amateur wrestler/boxer

Coach Funk does a nice job of laying out the organic nature of wrestling that gave birth to boxing and which maintains to this day such a stark contrast between the parent art of wrestling and its fistic offspring.

The religious beliefs that buoyed ancient Greek society were multi-layered traditions of ancestor worship. The eldest gods were the titans, earth deities worshipped by the original agrarian [farm-based] inhabitants of Hellas. Among the eldest of the titans was Uranus who was credited with being an all-out ground wrestler. The most powerful titan was Kronos, who gave his name to the hill overlooking the Altis at Olympia, where he was supposedly defeated in wrestling by Zeus [*Thunder-chief*], who was the chief of the Olympian gods; deities imported by the Indo-European nomads who were the ancestors of the dominant Greek tribes. Proteus [*First-chief*] was a lesser titan from Egypt, who supposedly fathered monstrous sons who were killed in wrestling by Herakles [*Hera's-honor*], who was the half mortal bastard son of Zeus. The minor Olympian god Hermes, god of athletic conduct, and his daughter Palaistra [*Wrestling-ground*] were also patrons of the wrestling arts. The gods of wrestling were both more ancient and more numerous than the gods of boxing. And boxing, patronized by Apollo, god of excellence, may rightly be viewed as a refinement of the primal art of wrestling. Many heroes and minor demigods such as Peleus, father of Achilles, Atalanta, the Amazon who out-wrestled Peleus, Jason, captain of the Argo, and Theseus [*Thought-lord*], slayer of the Bull of Minos, were essentially patron-saints of wrestling.

Furthermore, the fact that Hellenic wrestling was a stand-up art hints at an origin among nomads, whose wrestling arts generally involve little ground work, as even being on the ground was thought to be a *demeaning* state among people who lived their lives on horseback or being drawn by horse in a chariot.

The last in the long line of wrestling gods was a historical figure, Hipposthenes [*Horse-strong*] of Sparta, to whom the people of Lakonia [*The Silent Land*] raised a temple after his death. The ancient Greeks were a pre-scientific people—as most modern folks are post-scientific people, just as liable to adopt a superstitious outlook as were the ancients—for whom the world was more easily understood when its unseen powers were vested with human attributes, and to whom humans with amazing attributes were more easily appreciated as divinely gifted than as mundanely successful. In a world without health insurance, antibiotics and the many promises of scientific discoveries to come, every amazing life lived was a beacon of hope that people did not willingly forget. When one believes that life ends in a descent to a dusty hell, than the transient victories of the living tend to be faithfully immortalized, in the hopes that someday, another's life will be less bitterly lived by way of some victory yet to be won.

Archaic Wrestling & Spartan Supremacy: 708 to 540 B.C.

"Near is a temple of Hipposthenes [*Horse-strong*], who won so many victories in wrestling. They [the Spartans] worship Hipposthenes in accordance with an oracle, paying him honors as to Poseidon [god of horses, earthquakes and the sea]."
   -Pausanias, *Lakonia*

   708 B.C.: Wrestling is introduced at the 18th Olympiad.

> "Of those who dare, a strong-bound band,
>   Braced for battle, their *arete* as one,
> Grappling with the enemy, hand to hand,
>   Few shall die of wounds, in the dust."
>   -Tyrtaeus, *War Songs*

   668 B.C.: Tyrtaeus, a plodding, blood-thirsty Spartan poet, became famous for cheering the fearsome, though outnumbered grunts of Sparta on to battle, in the wake of their crushing defeat by the Argives at Hysaie. The Argive-Spartan rivalry

spanned athletics, dueling and war, and Tyrtaeus admonished his listeners not to forsake the duty of slaughter for the joys of wrestling. To read this testosterone-laden propaganda disguised as art is mind-numbing to the modern mind, but apparently had its desired effect...

650 B.C.: Spartan warriors crushed their Messenian slaves in battle. Some of the Messenian fugitives migrated to the island of Rhodes and founded a ruling family that would produce one of the greatest prize-fighters of all time—who was destined to die for fighting the Spartans.

632 B.C.: Introduction of boys' running & wrestling at the 37th Olympiad. Hipposthenes of Sparta wins boys' wrestling. The Sicilian Greek Orikadamos [*Bringing-order-to-subduing*] defined wrestling technique.

628 B.C.: Introduction of boys' pentathlon at Olympia. Eutelidas [*Good-?*] of Sparta wins the boys' wrestling & pentathlon. The Eleans abolish the boys' pentathlon.

624 B.C.: Hipposthenes wins wrestling at the 39th Olympiad. Draco passes "draconion" laws at Athens.

620 B.C.: Hipposthenes wins wrestling at the 40th Olympiad.

616 B.C.: Hipposthenes wins wrestling at the 41st Olympiad.

612 B.C.: Hipposthenes wins wrestling at the 42nd Olympiad.

608 B.C.: Hipposthenes wins wrestling at the 43rd Olympiad.

604 B.C.: Hetoemokles [*Prepared-for-honor*], of Sparta, son of Hipposthenes, wins wrestling at the 44th Olympiad, probably at the age of 21or 22.

600 B.C.: Hetoemokles wins wrestling at the 45th Olympiad. The Dioskureia agon is founded at Sparta. The stone temple of Hera and the Bouleuterium are built at Olympia.

596 B.C.: Hetoemokles wins wrestling at the 46th Olympiad. The Prytaneum is built at Olympia.

592 B.C.: Hetoemokles wins wrestling at the 47th Olympiad.

589 B.C.: An inscription is carved by Greek mercenaries serving in Egypt.

588 B.C.: Hetoemokles wins wrestling at the 48th Olympiad.

576 B.C.: The Spartans are upset at the 51st Olympiad, never to regain their dominance.

572 B.C.: The Eleans destroy the Pisans [co-promoters of the Olympics] and expand the Olympic truce.

553 B.C.: Construction of the Olympic stadium.

552 B.C.: The wrestler and/or diskus thrower Bybon threw a 315 pound stone overhead with one hand! The boulder is of red sandstone, and measures 2 feet 3 inches, by 1 foot 1 inch and 1 foot 3 inches.

548 B.C.: The insane battle of the 600 champions was fought between the Argives and Spartans at Thyrea. The lone Spartan survivor, Othryades, raised the victory trophy. Some years later Othryades fought a duel against Perilaus [*For-*

the-people] of Argos, a Nemean wrestling victor, and was killed.

545 B.C.: The Parparonia agon is founded at Sparta.

c.540 B.C.: The Temple of Hipposthenes and the statue of Hetoemokles were probably raised in the sacred precinct of Sparta at this time in response to the raising of statues at Olympia. The Spartan wrestlers Seleadas [*Bright-torch*] and Kalliteles [*Beautifully-complete*] won victories in boys' Olympic wrestling at some point after this date, but probably failed to win as men because of the dominance of Milo of Kroton.

*Note: Spartan may be translated as *rope-maker*. The warriors of Sparta referred to themselves as Lakadaemons [*Men-of-the-Silent-Land*].

Figure 50.

Like Roof-Timbers

Attic Amphora, by Nikosthenes, 530 B.C.

This scene is from the back belly of the vase from which figures 44 and 45 were drawn [*The Gods of Boxing*]. The wrestler on the left has a cauliflower ear and is digging into the earth with his lead left foot. The instances of lead left-feet in wrestling further suggest a wrestling origin for boxing, where the lead left is the rule. Both fighters are pushing off with their rear legs. The fighter on the right has the upper hand in this clinch and has foiled the left fighter's attempt to pummel his hip by grabbing the wrist. However, things are not all going his way as his opponent has grabbed his right forearm and is contesting the neck-hold.

Such bouts may have stagnated in such a reference point for long moments. In modern times there are tales of Turkish wrestlers clinching for hours and even days! However, as Homer hinted in *The Iliad*, there was considerable social pressure on ancient Greek wrestlers to go for the throw. And they may have been encouraged by the forked rod of the judge.

All-Power-Fighting

The rules for Greek wrestling were simple enough. There was no striking, gouging or biting allowed—finger-breaking was frowned upon but tolerated. The first wrestler to throw his opponent three times cleanly was the victor. A clean throw meant a toss that landed the opponent on his torso from any point from hip to shoulder. If both wrestlers went down nothing was counted. Apparently, wrestlers were also permitted to submit their opponents through locks or chokes; if so those who submitted were probably eliminated without the need for additional attempts to throw one-another.

The Age of Milo of Kroton: 542 to 510 B.C.

542 B.C.: Milo [*Sheep*], son of Diotimus [*Heavenly-honor*] of Kroton wins boy's wrestling at the 9th Pythiad.

540 B.C.: Milo wins boy's wrestling at the 60th Olympiad.

538 B.C.: Milo wins wrestling at the 10th Pythiad.

Legend attributed Milo's great strength to a diet that included eating the gizzard stones of roosters.

537 B.C.: Milo wins wrestling at the Nemean agon.

536 B.C.: Milo wins wrestling at the Isthmus in spring and at Olympia in late summer.

535 B.C.: Milo wins wrestling at Nemea.

534 B.C.: Milo wins wrestling at the Isthmus and the 11th Pythiad.

Milo was supposedly capable of bursting a cord tied around his head by inhaling and expanding his veins.

533 B.C.: Milo wins wrestling at Nemea.

532 B.C.: Milo wins at the Isthmus. At the
62nd Olympiad [a likely date] all of the other
wrestlers refused to compete against Milo. He was
summoned to be crowned immediately. But he
slipped and fell on his back, and the crowd shouted
for him to be denied the crown for the fall. As he
rose Milo said, "That was not the third fall, I fell
once. Let someone throw me the other times." He
was crowned without a single tussle.

531 B.C.: Milo is victorious at Nemea.
Milo was famous for lifting a 4-year-old cow.
According to Phylarkhus he ate an entire bull
before the altar of Zeus. Theodorus recorded that
Milo once ate 20 loaves of bread with an equal
amount of meat and washed it down with 3 gallons
of wine. The most likely of the Milo eating legends
was told by the historian Alexander of Aetolia, who
claimed that the Aetolian wrestler Titormos [?]
defeated Milo in a beef-eating contest. The fact that
both men were shepherds may have accounted for
their preferring a meat diet.

530 B.C.: Milo is victorious at the Isthmus
and at the 12th Pythiad.

529 B.C.: Milo is victorious at Nemea.

528 B.C.: Milo is victorious at the Isthmus
and at the 63rd Olympiad

527 B.C.: Milo is victorious at Nemea.
Milo was famous for a feat of strength in which he
held his right arm by his side, elevated his forearm
thumb side up, and extended his fingers. People
were then unable to bend back his small finger.

526 B.C.: Milo is victorious at the Isthmus and at the13th Pythiad.

525 B.C.: Milo wins at Nemea.

524 B.C.: Milo wins at the Isthmus and the 64th Olympiad.

523 B.C.: Milo wins at Nemea.

522 B.C.: Milo wins at the Isthmus and at the 14th Pythiad.

521 B.C.: Milo wins at Nemea.

520 B.C.: Milo wins at the Isthmus and at the 65th Olympiad.
Xenophanes, a philosopher from Kolophon, argues against rewarding athletes with material prizes.

518 B.C.: Milo wins at the Isthmus and at the 15th Pythiad.

516 B.C.: Milo struggles in the final match at the 66th Olympiad against Timasitheon, a young wrestler from Kroton, who uses the boxing technique known as "high-handedness" to avoid the clinch. Milo was not thrown once, or even took a knee. So the prize must have been dedicated to Zeus.

512 B.C.: The Sybarites establish an agon at Sybaris in competition with the 67th Olympiad, and attempt to bribe athletes to attend their agon instead of competing at Olympia.

Milo retires and carries his own bronze statue into the Altis. Milo's likeness, sculpted by Dameas, stood on a diskus-like base and held a pomegranate in his hand. Pausanias claimed that Milo used to stand on a greased diskus and challenge people to knock him off, and that he could hold a pomegranate in one hand, and that no one could pry even a finger loose, and that the fruit would not be harmed by his grip.

510 B.C.: Milo leads an army of 10,000 Krotians against an army of 30,000 Sybarites. He fights as a front-rank man, wearing his 6 Olympic crowns, and a lion skin and wielding a great club in imitation of Herakles. He is assisted by Dorieus [*Spear-chief*] of Sparta, an exiled son of a Spartan King. The Sybarite army is routed and their city is destroyed.

Milo lived the remainder of his days as an influential member of the Pythagorean circle of Kroton, and various legends attest to his close relationship to Pythagoras, perhaps being a son-in-law to the philosopher.

Figure 51.

Pentathletes Wrestling

Carving on marble base from Athens, c.510 B.C.

The pentathlete to the left is in the take-off position for the sprint.

The smaller wrestler has seized the larger wrestler's left forearm with both hands, and is possibly attempting to turn in and execute a shoulder-throw. The larger wrestler is checking his opponent's move by pressing his right hand against the smaller man's left shoulder.

The figure on the right is adjusting the strap on his javelin in preparation for a cast.

This carving either suggests wrestling practice out in the gymnasium, or running [presumably under the covered track] and javelin casting [presumably at a target] in the palaestra. The later is most likely, as the opposite carving on this base [Figure 61.] does represent a palaestra scene.

Classical Wrestling 508 to 401 B.C.

c. 508 B.C.: Demokedes, foremost physician of the time, escapes from the agents of the Persian King, to whom he is a personal slave. When agents of the Great King came to his home city of Kroton to plead for his return, they were rebuffed by the ruling council. Before the Persians left Kroton Demokedes told them to inform their King that he was engaged to marry the daughter of Milo—a privilege that cost him a small fortune. It was said that Demokedes sought this marriage in order to impress the King with his importance at home, since the King was known to be an admirer of Milo.

c.500 B.C.: The Athenian wrestler Telemakhos [*Complete-fighter*] kills an opponent, probably at the PanAthenia, and is cleared of responsibility for the other wrestler's death. ?Leontiskos [*Lion-great-?*] of Messene wins two Olympic victories by bending his opponents' fingers back until they snap.

"Eumastas [*Fair-eater?*], son of Kritobolos [*Chosen-stone*], lifted me from the ground."

-inscription on 1200 pound stone found on Thera

"I am no wrestler of Messene or Argos. Sparta, famous for her men, is my city. Those others are skilled in the art, but I, as a boy of The Silent Land, conquer through strength."
-Simonides, a victory epitaph at Olympia for Damagetus [*Submission-unwilling*]

"...the dexterous charioteer of wrestling..."
-Simonides, from a victory epitaph at Olympia for Theognetus [*Priest-?*]

c.490 B.C.: Milo is killed in some sort of farming or land-clearing accident, which is later expanded into a an unflattering fable that cast him as a witless fool, despite the fact that he was academically and politically connected with the leading men of his day.

Simonides defeats Askhylus in a poetry contest with an elegy for those who fell fighting at Marathon. Askhylus goes on to compose various famous works studded with wrestling metaphors...

"Our life is wrestlings" -*Suppliants*

"...such a wrestler he is now prepared for himself." -*Prometheus Bound*

"...limbs capable of tripping up even swift runners..." -*Eumenidius*

"Many wrestlings that weight down the limbs, with the knee pressing into the dust."
-*Oresteia*

480 B.C.: Theopompus, son of Theopompus the pentathlete of Argos, wins wrestling at the 75th Olympiad.

476 B.C.: An athlete of Maroneia won at the 76th Olympiad.

472 B.C.: [...]menes of Samos defeats the men, and [...]kratidas of Taras the boys at the 77th Olympiad.

468 B.C.: Theaeus [*Spectacle-chief*] of Argos wins at the Isthmus. At the 78th Olympiad Ephamostus [*Famed-for-cunning*] of Opus wins wrestling, and [...]emos of Parrhasia boy's wrestling.

467 B.C.: Theaeus wins at Nemea.

466 B.C.: Theaeus wins at the Isthmus and in the Pythiad at Delphi.

464 B.C. Theaeus wins at Isthmus. Pherias [?] of Aegina defeats boys at the 79th Olympiad

463 B.C. Alkimidas [*Mighty-virile?*] of Aegina defeats the boys at Nemea.

460 B.C.: Alkimidas defeats the boys at the 80th Olympiad.

456 B.C.: Alkimidas defeats the men at the 81st Olympiad.

Note: Possible mid-century Olympic champions in men's wrestling include Kheimon [*Winter*] of Argos, Baukis [?] of Trezen, and Taurosthenes [*Bull-strong*] of Aegina.

The dominant wrestler of the 450s was probably Pythodelos [?] of Athens who appears not to have travelled to Olympia to compete. His victories totaled 2 Pythian, 5 Isthmian, and 7 Nemean.

The dominant wrestler of the late 440s was Aristomenes [*Best-abider*] of Aegina who did one sweep of the circuit, with one win each at Olympia, Pythia, Isthmus and Nemea.

c.440 B.C.: The Athenian clown Eudikus becomes popular for his imitations of wrestlers and boxers.

Note: Wrestling records for the last quarter of the 5th Century are vague. Dominant youth wrestlers probably included Agenor [?] of Thebes; Euthymenes [*Fair-abider*] of Maenalus; Xenokles [*Friend's-honor*] of Maenalus; and Alexenikos [*Protector-of-victory*] of Elis; who were all Olympic victors.

Classical Wrestling from 400 to 323 B.C.

"A weak man is but a step removed from a sickly man...Parts that have been exercised resist change, being stronger than otherwise, and therefore less liable to waste."
    -Hippokrates, *Nutriment*, c. 400 B.C.

400 B.C.: Hippias of Elis compiles The *Olympic Register*, tracing victors back to 776 B.C.
    372 B.C.: Symmakhus [*Fellow-fighter*] of Elis wins boy's wrestling at the 102nd Olympiad.
    371 B.C.: The Thebans under Epaminondas crush the Spartans at the Battle of Leuktra in July. The First Century B.C. Roman historian, Cornelius Nepos, later discussed how the military reforms Epaminondas had instituted included reality-based military wrestling:

"...he aimed less at strength than agility...he trained himself thoroughly in running and wrestling, but he practiced wrestling only to the extent of being able, while still standing, to seize his opponent and contend with him."

The statement above is very important in understanding the value of wrestling as an ancient preparation for heavy infantry combat. Also, at this time, the Sparatan kings had no Olympic wrestling victors to stand by their side in the line of battle.

370 B.C.: Kudeides [?] of Athens wins men's wrestling at the Eleusinia [a minor agon].
Note: The Eleans appear to dominate boy's wrestling throughout the 4th Century with victories by Lysippus [?], Anaukhidas [?], Pherenicos [?-victor], Philles [Lover?], and Euanoridas [?] Other victors in boys Olympic wrestling include Eikasios [?] and Hermesianax [?] of Kolophon, Nikostratos [Victor-in-war] of Heraea, Kratinos [Power-?] of Aegeira, and Prokles [First-honor] of Andros [Manly-isle] known for its strong wrestlers.

362 B.C.: The death of Epaminondas at the Battle of Mantinea, in which his force was victorious.

356 B.C.: The probable date for the first Olympic victory of Khairon [With-impunity] of Pellene, who would go on to win 3 more Olympic crowns. Khairon was said to be a pupil of Plato, as was Aristotle, the tutor of Alexander of Makedon. This is a likely date in terms of Khairon's age, as well as his renown among the Makedonian leadership, who would eventually retain his political services. It was at this, the 106th Olympiad, that Phillip of Makedon would win the horse race.

350 B.C.: Xenokles [Friend's-honor] of Athens wins boy's wrestling at Athens.

338 B.C.: The Makedonian army under Phillip and Alexander crush the forces of the Greek alliance at the Battle of Khaeronei.

336 B.C.: The probable date on which Khilon [*Forager*] of Patrae won the first of his two Olympic victories. It was on this year that Alexander [*Protector-of-men*] of Makedon succeeded his murdered father to the throne, and commissioned statues of his family at Olympia. It was also the year in which Alexander made the Olympic wrestler and philosophy student Khairon Tyrant of Pellene. Khairon and his memory were hated by the people of Pellene down to the time of Pausanias, some 500 years later.

323 B.C.: After the death of Alexander in Babylon an outclassed rebel Greek army marched against the Makedonian army of Antipater, with Khilon of Patrae fighting as a promakhus [*front-rank-fighter*]. In the wake of this costly defeat Khilon was buried at public expense by the Akhaeans. Below is the inscription on his statue at Olympia*.

"Alone-wrestling victorious at Olympia & Pythia twice
        among the men,
        at Nemea thrice-wrestling & at the Isthmus four-wrestlings,
        Khilon, son of Khilon of Patrae, by the people Akhaean,
        for valiant battle-death honored by burial."

*Translated by the author.

As always, Khilon's biographer, Pausanias, had great sympathy for those Greeks who had died fighting in defense of their homeland. He had this to say about Khilon the wrestler:

"...his courage caused him to be the lone Akhaean to fight against Antipater's Makedonians at the Battle of Lamia in Thessaly."

Khilon, the Olympic wrestling champion, died a war hero.

Balls of Thunder: Body-Building & Chemistry in Ancient Times

"I could get this big naturally. But I'm an American and I want it now—so I use [steroids & growth hormones]. But the hardest part is eating all of this shit! You wouldn't believe what I eat."
-Rick Wayne, bodybuilder, 1989

In ancient times much was made by numerous historians and philosophers of the appetites and eating habits of wrestlers and all-power-fighters. The record is curiously silent on the pure boxers, so we may assume a balanced body-building diet for boxers since they had no need to make weight, as there were no weight classes in ancient times. To understand the apparent eating disorders of ancient strong men such as Milo and Astyanax we must appreciate the two primary roots of Indo-European prize-fighting: the hunt-feast, and wrestling. Hunting is the oldest human activity and wrestling the oldest sport attested to in prehistoric art. Hunting is the source of feasting among nomads and wrestling is the form of ritual combat most combatable with such high cohesion activities as hunting and feasting, as well as an art revered by Eurasian nomads.

Among peoples who had traversed the steppes corridor from Northeast Asia to the Near East and Europe, feasting on great quantities of meat was a tradition. In fact, great warriors into the middle ages, such as Babyrs the Mameluke warlord [famed for his ability to eat an entire lamb] were renowned for their appetites. In such warlike societies feasting was often enshrined as a contest. Therefore it is no surprise that ancient scholars addressed the eating of unusual quantities of food. But was there more to the diets of such men as Milo and Polydamas than ritual gluttony? Did the athletes of the past seek victory through the use of animal hormones and body-building agents just as modern scientists, body-builders and baseball players have?* Or were they simply indulging the compulsive eating disorders that still plague boxers of the 21st Century?**

It is not uncommon among primitives for hunters and warriors to consume the choice organs of their prey or enemy, in the superstitious hope of acquiring an attribute associated with that organ or individual. There has been some discussion among modern strongmen—who often inject growth hormones—as to whether or not the modern practice of eating "mountain oysters" [the testicles of bulls, pigs or rams] is a remnant of an ancient form of hormone supplementation. A reading of Milo's eating habits points towards experimentation at least. And, if the most dominant athlete in sports history ate animal parts, it is almost certain that the practice—whether it began with him or not—would have spawned numerous imitators.

As the effects of the loss of testicles on men and livestock were well-known among the ancients—who took care not to neuter their warhorses—and included loss of strength and aggressiveness, then they may have logically looked to the testicles of the sacrificial bull for added strength. While following this line of inquiry we must not forget the central significance of the bull cult and Indo-European ritual. Just as modern trainers believe that a severe depletion of sperm prior to a fight will weaken a fighter, the trainer of Promakhus of Pellene was said to have talked him out of intercourse with his young love prior to his bout with Polydamas. Although there is no direct evidence that ancient fighters consumed animal hormones as a body-building aid, there remains much in the record to indicate the likelihood of such a practice.

Although the consumption of "natural steroids" to enhance performance among ancient athletes must remain a subject of speculation, we can be certain of the character of such an act, if it had been a common practice. If Milo, Astyanax, Polydamas, or any of the other mutant jocks of antiquity consumed animal testicles to enhance their performance, they would have done so under the supervision of a priest and a trainer, and the act would have been a sacral one, probably at the altar of Zeus where one swore his agonistic oath, or in the sanctuary of Zeus' mighty bastard Herakles where one prayed for victory.

*Dunning, A.J. *Extremes: Reflections in Human Behavior*, Harcourt Brace Jovanovich, NY, 1992, pages 102-13
   This piece opens with an interesting discussion of an aging 19th Century scientist injecting himself with testicular animal extracts.

**Goodman, Margaret. *Eating Disorders in Boxing*, The Ring, #5, 2005, page 126
   According to Goodman, while 11% of women and only 1% of men suffer from eating disorders, 10% of male athletes are afflicted with this behavior, for which boxers are noted.

Comparing Ancient & Modern Fighters

I have written this book for the modern fighter in order to connect him with the roots of his art—roots he may not have known existed. This is also a book for the fight fan, who will naturally ask the question, "Could these guys hang with today's fighters?"

Of course the fighter reading this book has already internalized this same question, so I knew going in that I would need to develop a process for objectively comparing ancient and modern fighters. Debates along this line emerge periodically in boxing and martial arts magazines, with the participants taking sides for or against the fighters of the past.

There are three underlying flaws to this dialog structure, which dooms the debate to irrelevance from the outset:

1. *Linear thinking.* Both sides argue along a direct linear path to the past. Some will say that mankind continually improves in all pursuits, therefore modern fighters are

better, while others argue the "old-timers"
are made of tougher stuff –a "stuff"
that can never be captured by modern
athletes weaned on luxury foods. Both sides
of this debate structure had counterparts
among ancient thinkers, which buttresses this
author's contention that fighting arts evolve
and devolve according to cyclic
rhythms, and that a linear model is
fundamentally flawed.

2. *A subjective worldview* is one which
dooms the debater to consider all things from
his limited field of experience, depriving him
of a true understanding of the subject. To
debate ancient versus modern you must be
able to understand the ancient context as well
as the modern. This is why I have developed
this sub-study, so that those considering the
inevitable question of Klitchko versus
Theogenes will at least be able to consider the
world from the perspective of Theogenes.

3. *Ignorance of combat,* will afflict most who
take up a debate without having actual
experience or true knowledge of one of the
activities being argued. Many fight fans have
no experience of combat and most fighters
have a limited perspective. For this reason
experimentation with ancient fighting
methods without resorting to the martial
crutch of choreography is necessary. As the
author of this study I have thus gained
experience in all of these areas to provide

myself with some insight. Basically it comes down to the following equation:

> The old-time bare-knuckle fighter of the 18th 7 19th centuries was the toughest

> The modern fighter is the biggest, strongest & fastest

> The ancient fighter was a product of "old-time" & "modern" athletic trends which coexisted in his time over a vast period, resulting in a combat athlete who would have had a fair chance in a bare-knuckle fight, a modern gloved boxing bout, or post-modern mixed-martial arts cage fight.

>All three of these athletic models were developed to compete in "their sphere" but the ancient fighter was the product of a longer more open tradition, and therefore more adaptable. Bare-knuckle fighters just didn't possess the fire-power to compete with today's fighters, and modern fighters don't possess the finesse & raw toughness to survive without gloves, but the ancient fighter practiced an art that required all of these assets.

What follows is the formula I developed for coming to these generalized conclusions...

The Eight Contexts of Ritual Combat

1. *Genetic*
2. *Dietary*

3. *Demographic*
4. *Technological*
5. *Cultural*
6. *Linguistic*
7. *Ritual Absolutes*
8. *Ritual Parameters*

The first 3 contexts help us establish the physical makeup of a fighter type, while 4 through 6 are tools for establishing the social structure within which the athlete developed and competed, and 7 and 8 establish points of comparison concerning the actual types of combat engaged in.

1. *Genetic*
   The body-type of a fighter is largely pre-determined, and certain body-types are ideal for certain types of combat. An art developed by Eskimos will be much different than that developed by Nilotic [tall Saharan] Africans. The sculpture, pottery art, and poetry of the ancient world—along with knowledge of common body-types among Greco-Roman descendents today—is indispensable for this aspect of our study.

2. *Dietary*
   People point to the tiny uniforms of American civil war soldiers and the armor of feudal Japanese samurai and make statements such as, "people were tiny before modern times", and go on to assume that humans of the past

were all impossibly tiny. Even the old-time heavyweight boxers of the 20th century are regarded as small by 21st century standards. So it obviously follows that the Greeks and Romans were anorexic midgets, right? Wrong.

Nutritional intake during childhood is a great variable in determining adult stature, and the nutritional intake of a developing athlete is a huge component in determining his mass and the development of fast-twitch muscle fibers. The question is what kind of diet did the ancient fighters benefit from? The answer is one of a quality second only to that which can be provided by the 21st century global super-economy. Feudal societies are generally poorly nourished at all social levels. Early industrial societies have undernourished masses of poor and well-fed rich. A 19th century British officer might be a full 6 inches taller than the mass of men he commanded who grew up on a low-protein diet in the slums of Wales while he dined on the produce of his family estate. Agrarian slave societies such as Greece and Rome also had poorly nourished under-classes, but their middle- and upper-class members were better nourished than their counterparts of the industrial age. And finally, cattle-herding and hunting societies—who produced the first prize-fighters—had extremely high-protein diets that might even make a modern-day body-builder gag. Again, we are looking at cyclic social patterns.

3. *Demographic*

   There are a lot more people on the world today, and modern athletes are drawn from such an ethnically diverse collection of global communities that the ancient Greco-Roman talent pool would seem shallow indeed. This is a good point. So, if it is such a good point why doesn't it establish the rule? Yes, we have a much larger pool of potential athletes today, but they are spread across dozens of pro sports while the ancient Greeks had only a single dozen events and the Romans pretty much dropped all but 5: chariot racing, monomakhia, pankration, boxing & wrestling. But even with the modern athletes spread over 4 times the events—many of them being team sports which causes a further thinning of the human resources—Greece and Rome were only drawing from a small area of the world, not globally, so the talent pool is still vastly larger today. However, the typical modern male engages in no martial activity or sport, while all of the men of ancient Greece trained in combat sports, and all of the suitable slaves of the pretty massive Roman Empire were fed into the arena. I will still give the nod to today's larger talent pool on the ground that raw talent tends to rise above the masses, and bigger numbers means more raw talent. But remember that the very best athletes of ancient times would never play ball, they would fight.

4. *Technological*
   This is certainly a concern for the gladiator of yesterday and the football player of today, but it also determines the behavior of boxers. Basically you can do 5 things with the fist to prepare it for your ritual combat:
   1. nothing
   2. brace it
   3. wrap it
   4. armor it
   5. glove it

   Choosing to do any of the above will affect the behavior of your boxers to such a degree that the event itself becomes uniquely enmeshed in a web of apparent and subtle technical parameters. Your best chance of adapting to another method would really be based on how many steps removed from your own art it is on the table above. Switching from bare-knuckle to armored boxing or visa-versa would likely be a disaster. But one step on the tech scale is not so bad. The technology of hand coverage gives the "wrapped" *pugmakhos* of ancient Greece the best chance to adapt to the widest variety of events, while gloved and bare-knuckle fighters face the greatest technical hurdles.

5. *Cultural*
    What is the relationship of the fighter to civil society, military society, sacred society, and criminal society? What pressures do politics, warfare, religion and crime place on the prize-fighter. How could these pressures affect his behavior?

6. *Linguistic*
    What clues to the cultural importance of the prize-fighting art and its practice are indicated in the linguistic record?

7. *Ritual Absolutes*
    What is absolutely required of the participant? Must he be free? Criminal? Naked?
    Uniformed? Must he bow to or shake hands with his opponent? How might adherence to these absolutes effect training and combat?

8. *Ritual Parameters*
    What limits do the rules of combat place on the individual? Must he fight in a restricted space? What technologies and techniques may he employ? What are the conditions for victory?

Each of the above 8 contexts raises multiple points of comparison. Once you begin to delve deeply into these layers of questions and comparisons your opinions will be challenged, and your perspective will be broadened. The construction of and respect for such a formula as a tool of inquiry can be very enlightening; but don't let it turn into an academic water-torture, have fun with it and let it feed your curiosity.

The Alternative Warrior: Homosexuality and Martial Culture

"Such [homosexual] attachments were not merely tolerated, they were encouraged, in what was predominantly a male society, as being conductive to comradeship and self-sacrifice on the battlefield."
-Stephen Turnbull, *Samurai Warlords: The Book of the Daimyo*

"...you low-life! You meet my son just as he comes out of the gymnasium, all fresh from the bath, and you don't kiss him, don't say a word to him, you don't hug him, you don't even feel his balls! And yet you are supposed to be our friend!"
-Aristophanes, *Birds*

Above we have two examples of homosexual practices among the ruling class of warlike societies. Academics have put forth a wide range of views concerning the Greek practice. There is little or no documentation concerning sexual activities in the majority of Greek communities. Most of our information comes from Athenian and Alexandrian sources, and these report primarily on the activities of the rich in Athens and Alexandria, and give second-hand accounts concerning the homosexual practices in Sparta, Krete, and Thebes. In most cases these practices seem to be limited sexual engagements between men and adolescents. Perhaps one third of Spartan men actually had sexual relations with their mentors. Among the Athenians the practice seemed primarily an aristocratic one. The Kretans were reputed to be sex-fiends from whom even their mountain goats were not safe, and some of what went on in Alexandria brings to mind the escapades of 20th Century Catholic priests abusing altar boys. However, all of this activity falls within the realm of bi-sexual behavior. Only the 150 members of the famous Theban Sacred Band, which constituted 75 married pairs, seemed to have engaged in homosexual behavior as it is understood in 21st Century America.

The modern perception, as depicted in the 2005 movie *Alexander*, that ancient Greek warriors were a bunch of butt-buddies is very far from the mark. Granted it's a mark that has long ago been lost in the mists of time, though it is one that can be understood through the examination of male-on-male sexual relationships among other martial peoples, such as the Japanese. Prolonged barracking and campaigning among warriors who are often denied the company of women does result in an unusually high rate of sexual activity between males. This is also true in extremely abusive institutions such as English boarding schools and Royal Navy ships of the Victorian and Georgian era as well as in modern prisons. When periods of endemic conflict span generations, such as in feudal Japan, than the practice of battle-field mentoring may become tied up with the notion of man-boy-love. As disgusting as this potentially abusive relationship seems to the modern conscience, it was often viewed as conducive to good battle-field cohesion by pre-industrial martial societies that suffered from political fragmentation and endemic small-scale warfare. Krete seems to have been the most extreme example of this type of social structure in ancient Greece.

What does this inquiry into male bisexuality mean to our inquiry into the life of the ancient boxer? Some writers express the opinion that the nakedness of the ancient prize-fighter made sexual activity between men more likely. Again, nakedness seen through the eyes of a modern person warps perception of the ancient situation. Nakedness, when it is a normal state of being, is not the erotic morality-bender that it is in our own repressed world, where the fat masses keep themselves covered and nakedness is generally reserved for sexually charged expositions. In fact, in modern times, some of the few public viewing of naked [as naked as is socially acceptable] is in the combat sports of pro boxing and ultimate fighting.

One of the factors that has been put forward as an indication of sexual arousal in ancient prize-fighting was the use of the penis string used to tie the foreskin over the head of the placid penis before competition. The primary reason for this was probably to prevent sand and dirt from getting inside the foreskin. However, another effect of this procedure would have been the suppression of erections. Of course, this fact is taken as evidence that these men tended to get sexually exited while fighting naked and that this would be embarrassing. This is a ridicules assumption. Once again, a fighter's view will clear up most misconceptions about fighting. Some fighters do get erections when fighting, either because they are in a general state of arousal of are experiencing a pelvic floor cramp, or because they equate aggression with sex. For whatever the reason, this fighter will be in danger of having his erect penis broken if it is struck or bent. Another reason for tying a string the end of the penis would be to lengthen it and insure that it hangs in front of the more delicate testes, particularly the left one. A strike to the placid penis is rarely damaging.

The Real B.S.: Tall Tales & Ancient Greek Prize-fighters

"The aspect of the traditional portrait of Wallace with which critics and detractors had the least forbearance concerned his physical attributes.....But when we consider the circumstances in which he was placed, and the times in which he lived, we can see that these attributes were really essential to a leader of men, who had nothing but these very attributes to commend him."
        -James Mackay, *William Wallace: Brave Heart*

"Now I am obliged to record the statements made by the Hellenes, though I am not obliged to believe them all."
        -Pausanias, *Description of Greece*

Generally speaking, modern readers chose either to believe all the legends surrounding the athletes of antiquity, or reject all such heroic claims out of hand. The inquisitive mind should seek the truth somewhere between these two extremes, ideally using the insights of the authors quoted above as guides. The extraordinary physical feats ascribed to ancient combat athletes are limited to the Classical Period and fall into three categories: eating; strong-man stunts; and animal stunts.

The most widely ascribed feat is the eating of massive quantities of food. Some exaggeration may be expected, though it was probably not necessary. This author once interviewed the 4th ranked food-eating-competitor in the world. During the course of this interview I learned that the number one eater in the world was a 130 pound man who "trained like an athlete" for his competitions. Young men who have lived with roommates can often rattle off numerous tales of outrageously gluttonous behavior among their peers. In many pastoral societies the ability to consume great quantities of animal flesh is regarded as a sign of strength and vigor.

As the tens of thousands of modern viewers who have witnessed *The World's Strongest Man* events on ESPN2 can attest, the ability to perform feats of extreme strength—while dependent on natural and developed attributes—is often a matter of intelligently applied technique. In light of the incredible accomplishments of modern strength athletes there is nothing in the ancient record that defies belief.

The hardest stories to swallow are those that surround the person of Polydamas, who was reputed to have held back a chariot, man-handled a bull, and killed a lion with his bare hands. Based on the ability of average-sized modern rodeo pros to manhandle juvenile cattle, it should not astonish us that an extreme genetic freak whose home was the pastures of Thessaly would successfully abuse and thwart the efforts of domestic animals. The killing of a full-grown male lion by an unarmed man though, is hard to believe. Before looking into the details of Polydamas and the lion, we must keep in mind that these feats of his were essentially his attempt to emulate the mythical labors of Herakles; and that these labors were largely metaphors for mankind's mastery of nature. It should also be noted, that for virtually all of ancient history, the killing of lions was a privilege reserved for kings.

Polydamas' killing of a lion on the Thessalian slopes of Mount Olympus was commemorated on the base of his statue at Olympia, so the Eleans at least believed the tale to be authentic. One must also consider that Polydamas could have worn his proof to Olympia in the form of a lion-skin unmarred by arrow, spear, or sword. It was also the case that the Persian Emperor Darius and his agents believed that Polydamas had indeed killed such a lion bare-handed—this particular feat probably being the one that caught the ear of the Great King, who, like all Asiatic despots of the period, was certainly an avid lion-hunter, well qualified to quiz the giant concerning the details of his exploit. There are two more factors concerning the believability of Polydamas' strangulation of a fierce lion. Herakles was said to have slain the Nemean Lion with the aid of a massive club [and if Polydamas had beaten his lion with an olive-wood club, the hide would have been left intact]. Also, the Asiatic lion hunted by Polydamas was of a species

inferior in size to the African lion familiar to
modern people. It is therefore conceivable that the
giant ultimate-fighter faced a cat that was roughly
his size. Since there have been some documented
mid-20th Century cases in which big game hunters
in Africa and South America successfully fought off
big cats [a leopard—which the man killed by
shoving his arm down it's throat—and jaguar
respectively], than it is not impossible that
Polydamas strangled a lion. However, one does not
have to be a skeptic to assume that the venerable
house cat of the gods was only choked-out after
being worked over with a tree limb wielded by the
big man from Thessaly.

All-Power-Thing

Pankration from Lygdamis to Dioxippos, 648 to 325 B.C.

"...sweet forms wrapped in white robes,
   will go from the white-pathed earth and forsake
mankind to join the deathless gods:
   And bitter sorrows will be left for mortal men,
and there will be no help against evil."
   -Hesoid, *Works and Days*

Hesoid warned his listeners that the world would one-day return to a dark age of lawlessness; and they believed him. Their small civilized world was surrounded by vast lands roamed by barbarian tribes. Furthermore, the greatest folk-heroes of legend, the founders of the Greek town-nations, had been the sons of chaos. It was such a world that had produced the raging figure of Herakles [*Hera's-honor*], supposedly a bastard son of Zeus. Prize-fighters, war-fighters and kings all sacrificed to the brooding self-made figure of Herakles, for he represented the ultimate-fighter. With bow, spear, club, fist, throw or strangle-hold Herakles vanquished all of his enemies; and it was just such a man that people hoped to be led by in times of peril.

All-Power-Fighting

The pankration [*all-power-thing*] was instituted as a means of preserving this spirit among fighting men at the very time such all-round individuality in combat was being subverted by the need to maintain standardized citizen-militia forces. As the rich lazy nobles that ruled for centuries as the descendents of dark age war-chiefs were pushed aside by the hard-working farmer-soldier, the image of the war-chief was resurrected in the world of metaphor; in 648 B.C. the pankration was instituted at Olympia, and in 645 B.C. the age-old poem *The Labors of Herakles* was committed to writing by Peisander of Kamirus. Where wrestling, boxing and the pentathlon were each the province of many gods and heroes, the pankration was associated with the solitary figure of manly rage, Herakles [and, in Athens, with Theseus as well]. Before discussing his mythic labors we should make an inquiry into his actual life—for he surely lived.

The scholars of late antiquity recognized three legendary figures by the name of Herakles. Modern scholars suggest that the *Epic of Gilgamesh* provided the model for the *Labors of Herakles*. [Other Near Eastern heroes have also been suggested as Herakles prototypes.] However, this author believes that Gilgamesh and Herakles simply provided the same need and became the expression of political anxieties for two cultures separated by both time and space. The first Herakles may have been a pirate-chief that found his fame in the Nile delta as a mercenary for Egypt as early as 1700 B.C.

Around the year 1200 B.C. a Herakles of Thebes in central Greece was a notorious war-chief, and appears to have been the actual character about which the myths of Peisander and later authors were woven. It is of interest that central Greece had a strong connection with the Greek colonies in Egypt, and that one of the sacred cities of Pharonic Egypt was named Thebes. One is reminded of the legend of Benaiah [*The First Boxers*] and his Egyptian opponent. There was also a Herakles who immigrated from Crete and contributed one of the many starts or re-starts of the Olympic agon. The Theban Herakles—apparently the ultimate-fighter of his day—also held games at Olympia.

For a picture of the fighting-man envisioned by Peisander we must turn to the later [c.275 B.C.] Hellenistic author Theokritos: "...all the tricks and falls of the wrestlers of Argos, and of boxers skilled with the hand-strap, and all the cunning techniques of the all-power-fighters, these he learned from Harpalykos [*Seizing-wolf*] of Phanote, who no man could face confidently in the ring..."

Despite being outwitted by sleazy mortals and hated by his heavenly father's divinely jealous wife Hera [his existence as the bastard son of Zeus and the nymph Alkmene being the key to her soiled honor?] Herakles eventually triumphed over his mortal sorrows and came to be regarded as a god almost equal to his father Zeus and the rival of his half-brother Apollo, god of excellence.

All-Power-Fighting

The man who would eventually be worshipped by conquerors, emperors and gladiators was credited with the following combative feats: strangling a lion he had dazed with his well-balanced olive-wood club; killing the notorious head-butting bandit Termmerus [?] with a head-butt; killing the barbarian ogre Antaio by gouging out his eyes; killing the Sicilian hero Eryx in a boxing match; throwing a fat robber-king so hard that he split open like a sack; and prevailing in numerous duels and battles.

Herakles was famous for dressing in animal hides [indicating his great antiquity], and was addressed by such cult names as "ox-eater" and "nose-knocker". From Milo of Kroton to the Roman emperors, men who wielded power honored him as their patron god and went to great lengths to emulate his deeds and habits. During his march through Asia Alexander honored Herakles more often than the other gods, as he was a self-made god, as Alexander wished to be. He was also accompanied by an Olympic pankration champion who dueled with a club, in honor of Herakles.

His art, the pankration, was ultimately a forum for self-made men.

Archaic Pankration from Lygdamis to Phylakidas: 648 to 484 B.C.

> "Come to me now again; release me from
> Anxiety; accomplish all that my spirit
> Yearns to see accomplished; and you yourself
> Be my fellow-fighter."
>   -Sappho of Lesbos c.650 B.C.

In an age when a bi-sexual female poet evokes the image of combat in the context of a love song, one can easily imagine the hyper-aggressive nature of the dominant males who were her contemporaries.

648 B.C.: At the 33rd Olympiad horse racing [the things had finally been bred big enough to be ridden by men] and the pankration were introduced. The victor in the pankration was Lygdamis [*Twisting-subduer*] of Syracuse, who was reputed to be a giant with feet that measured a cubit [equal to the length from the elbow to extended finger-tip of a normal man].

645 B.C.: Peisander of Kamirus writes *The Labors of Herakles*.

644 B.C.: The King of Pisa, one of the three guardians of the Olympic truce, usurps the 34th Olympiad.

636 B.C.: Phrynon [*Torch-?*] of Athens wins the pankration at the 36th Olympiad.

608 B.C.: Phrynon serves as the general of an Athenian expedition to Lesbos and, at about the age of 50, and challenges the enemy general, the philosopher Pittakus of Mitylene, to single combat. Accepting the challenge, Pittakus conceals a net beneath his shield, and uses it to ensnare Phrynon, who he then kills.

592 B.C.: Anakharsis, half-Greek son of the King of the Skythian nomads, visits the house of Solon, boxer/politician of Athens, and discusses Greek athletics, the practice of which he finds astonishing. He is amazed that expert combatants contend at agons at which the prizes are awarded by non-experts; that law-givers impose penalties for civil assault but enumerate prizes to be gifted to prize-fighters for bruising one-another; and that body oil is a psychosis inducing drug because athletes become hyper-aggressive toward each other after anointing themselves before combat.

586 B.C.: Periander, Tyrant of Korinth, founds the Isthmian agon.

585 B.C.: Periander kicks his pregnent wife to death. Periander was the son of Kypselus, and it was he or his children who dedicated the chest of Kypselus to Zeus at his temple at Olympia [see Figure 36 in *The Gods of Boxing*.]

572 B.C.: The Eleans destroy Pisa and win control of the Olympics in time to celebrate the 52nd Olympiad, which is declared panHellenic [*for-all-Greeks*] like the newly instituted agons at Delphi, the Isthmus and Nemea. Arrikhion [*Earnest-snow*] of Phigalia is victor in the pankration.

568 B.C.: Arrikhion wins the pankration at the 53rd Olympiad.

566 B.C.: The PanAthenean agon is instituted at Athens.

564 B.C.: Arrikhion dies winning the pankration at the 54th Olympiad.

546 B.C.: Slaves are permitted to compete at the PanAthenea.

536 B.C.: The second statue ever dedicated for a victor in the Altis at Olympia is raised in honor of Rexibus [*Mighty-in-youth*] of Opunt for his victory in the pankration at the 61st Olympiad. This statue was set up next to the statue of Praxidamis the boxer near the pillar of Oenomaus [a notorious drunken chariot-racing king of pre-Olympian times], and was carved of figwood, which had decayed noticeably by the time of Pausanias' visit to the site 750 years later.

526 B.C.: Slaves are barred from competing in the PanAthenea.

501 B.C.: Themistius [?] of Aegina wins the boxing and the pankration at the agon at Epidauros. As Aegina was known for its strong stable of boxers it is likely that Themistius was a high-hand style boxer who managed to best a sub-Olympic quality

field of boxers and pankratiasts at this regional agon.

499 B.C.: Melesias of Athens beats the boys in the pankration at the Nemean agon.

497 B.C.: Melesias over the men in the Nemean pankration.

487 B.C.: Euthymenes of Aegina wins the pankration at Nemea. War between Athens and Aegina.

486 B.C.: Euthymenes [*Fair-abider*] wins the pankration at the Isthmian agon.

485 B.C.: Timodemos [*Honored-by-the-people*] of Akharnae wins the Nemean pankration.

484 B.C.: Phylakidas [*Guard-of-the-prize*] of Aegina wins the Isthmian pankration. The dominance of Aeginetans in the pankration at the Isthmian, Nemean and Epidaurian agons can be linked to two known facts: each of these agons were close to Aegina; and that boxing, at this date, was a viable pankration style.

Figure 92.

Arrikhion at Olympia

564 B.C.

Artist's conception based on the author's reading of Philostratus' description of a panoramic gallery painting and Pausanias' commentary on Arrikhion's statue at Phigalia

At about the age of 30 Arrikhion had returned to Olympia to compete for a third olive crown in the pankration. Fighting in the final round against his last remaining opponent [probably his third bout of the afternoon] Arrikhion was caught in a waist-lock from behind by the younger man. At this point his opponent went for the kill by way of the klimakismos [*ladder-trick*] hold: sliding his right forearm up into Arrikhion's throat and palming the back of his head and pushing down with the left as he wrapped his thighs around the standing fighter's waist, he was poised to finish the older fighter, on whom he was essentially riding "piggy-back".

The hold was finished by winding his lower legs through Arrikhion's thighs and hooking his feet around behind the knees, as he sunk in the choke. Arrikhion, obviously exhausted, since he had let a less experienced fighter around behind him, waited patiently for a mistake to be made. Just as he was losing consciousness due to the choke Arrikhion noticed that the younger fighter's foot hold about his knees had slackened. With his last effort he kicked out his right foot, reached around with his right arm and hooked the upper right leg, flexed his left knee to trap the opponent's left foot, and then fell heavily to his left, violently dislocating the other fighter's ankle.

This is the moment caught by the painter of the long vanished mural. Although dead, Arrikhion is still flushed with life as his spirit leaves his sweaty dust-covered body and his smiling corpse is crowned by the judge, as his living opponent seems pale as a corpse in his submissive state of agony— hand raised in defeat, and the crowd explodes with emotion: some jumping up from their folding chairs and shouting; some leaping from their seats on the ground; and still others slapping one another on the back.

Some 700 years later, when Pausanias passed through the market place of Arrikhion's home town of Phigalia, his statue still stood. His likeness was of stone, standing in an archaic pose [at attention] with his feet close together and his arms hanging by his side. Although statues have stood far longer with their carvings remaining legible, Pausanias informs us that the epigram on this statue had vanished with time. One wonders if it had been worn away by the admiring fingers of those who heard the story of Arrikhion's final victory. His statue was undoubtedly a favorite prayer spot for aspiring fighters.

The final consideration about this peerless athlete was his name, Earnest-snow. Was this the name he was known by throughout his life? Was it bestowed upon him as a commentary on his possible training among the mountains of his homeland? Or, perhaps, this was a name that he earned upon his death, indicating the earnestness of a heroic effort undertaken by a man in the winter of his agonal life?

Figure 93.

The Cruelest Kick

One-handled kantharos, 520 B.C.

The fighter on the left appears to have caught his larger advancing opponent cold with a front push kick. The injured fighter appears to have been stopped at the end of a long step. He seems to be guarding with his lead left hand while making the hand sign for submission with his right, which he has yet to raise to formally announce his defeat. The smaller fighter is accompanying his kick with a two handed push. The judge to the right seems to be signaling an end to the bout. The nature of the kick is not clear as it could be a push or snap kick. If it is a push kick [a foot jab] than the upper inside of the thigh or hip is being stuck with the heel or ball of the foot. If this kick were to the genitalia than it would be a snapping kick with the ball of the foot or shin bone. The pushing attitude of the kicker's hands are more combatable with a push kick than a snap kick. Although this may not be an attack on the genitalia, a heel stomp to the thigh just under the pelvis could also be debilitating.

Figure 94.

Kickboxing into the Clinch

from an Attic amphora, c.520B.C.

On this vase we have a dynamic fight seen officiated by the two perpetual observers of agonistic combat: the judge to the left and the trainer to the right. These two fighters are headed into a clinch, and a probable roll in the dust, as if by mutual agreement. The left fighter has committed with a posted foot jab which has been caught by his opponent's low lead hand. He is, however, scoring with his follow up blow, a posted plunging pronated jab to the heart, which is really going to hurt. His opponent seems set to counter with a straight right delivered as he lifts that leg—sending his man to his back—or after he steps in with his shoulder and dumps the kicker to his right side where he will drill him repeatedly with plunging rights. If the fighter to the right opts for this second counter than he may eat a vicious right punch to the chin or hammerfist to the neck or collar bone, either of which the kicker is chambered to deliver. If he just lifts that leg while he punches the kicker, things should go his way.

Points of interest include the attitude of the judge who appears to be signaling the start of the bout, which would indicate a real rivalry here, with

149

no preliminary circling. The trainer is obviously encouraging someone to punch.

The most noteworthy aspect of this piece is its intricacy. The kicker is shown at the terminus of a spent kick, at the apex of an effective jab, and chambered to throw a follow up blow. This single fighter is depicted simultaneously engaged in three techniques each in one of the three stages of execution. The fact that he is actively and effectively being engaged by a fighter who is employing a counter combination marks this as an extremely sophisticated representation of fluid combat. The pronated nature of the punches are unusual for the period and are probably used strictly to the body and chin, as they were in the modern bare-knuckle and small-glove period [A.D. c.1700 to c.1900].

Figure 95.

Elbowing Out of a Front Choke

from an Attic kelix fragment, late 6th Century B.C.

This seems to be the final stage of an extremely brutal encounter. The loser is fighting hard and the victor has pulled out all the stops by stepping on his man while he counters a feeble choke with a vicious elbow to set up a long uppercut which is going to further destroy the fallen man's profusely bleeding nose. Note the bloody right hand print on the downed fighter's chest. This indicates that the nose has been bleeding for a while, as this bloody hand print would have been made by a hand reaching around from behind, suggesting that the fight went to the ground due to a standing hip throw that may have been developed from a side waist-lock, with the now standing fighter having gotten in under his opponent's left arm and reached around behind to his opponent's right side with his own right hand before kicking the bleeding fighter's legs out and dumping him.

Everything about this scene, from the physiques, facial characteristics and tactical position indicates that the fighter with the upper hand is perceived as a dominant athlete and was destined to win this bout.

Figure 96.

The Monster Kickboxer

from a sketch of uncertain origin, possibly an Attic fragment c.510 B.C.

The fighter on the left is massive and this piece is laid out in such a way as to demonstrate his total dominance. The ill-fated hammerfist and uppercut being readied by his opponent are common boxing postures for the period and are entirely irrelevant to the action, which is one-sided in the extreme. The giant pankratiast is shielding with his lead left forearm as he simultaneously stomps on his opponent's thigh with an inside lead left heel kick and throws a straight vertical right punch to the heart. As soon as this combination— only effective against over-matched fighters—does its work, the monster kickboxer will be free to begin hammering away with lead hammerfists and rear-hand upper cuts.

The action is dutifully officiated by the familiar figure of the judge to the left [not depicted in this reproduction], who appears serenely

153

solemn, as if officiating over a preordained ceremony.

 Note: Figure 94 represents a contested application of this leg-kick body-punch combination against a fighter who has the tools to stop and counter it.

The Pankration from Hermolykos to Autolykos: 581 to 420 B.C.

"In the toiling of the clinch he was as bold as a lion, while in skill he was like the fox, who takes to her back to avoid the swoop of an eagle... For fate had not given him the strength of Orion, being small to the eye, but heavy in the grapple."
                    -Pindar, *4th Isthmian Ode: For Melissus of Thebes*

481 B.C.: Theogenes [*Priest-born*] of Thasos [*Woods-island*] wins the pankration at Nemea.

480 B.C.: Theogenes wins the boxing and pankration at the Isthmian agon. Later in the year he applies for the fist and the all-power-thing at the 75th Olympiad. After his boxing victory over Euthymus [*Grace-speaker*] he is too exhausted to fight the pankration; forfeiting to Dromeus [*Runner*] of Mantineia, who, being the only other pankratiast to enter—owing to the fearsome reputation of Theogenes—becomes the only pankratiast in history to take off the crown without

a single bout. The 300 Spartans die fighting the
Persian army at Thermopylae [*The-hot-gates*].

479 B.C.: The Athenian pankratiast
Hermolykos [*Hermes'-wolf*] distinguishes himself at
the battle of Mykale. [He later dies at the battle of
Kyrnos in Euboea.] The Greeks defeat the Persians
and Thebans at Plataea. The Eleatheria agon is
founded at Plataea to commemorate the victory and
the Epitaphia agon is founded at Athens to honor
the dead.

478 B.C.: Milissus [?] of Thebes wins the
pankration at the Isthmus and is praised by Pindar.

477 B.C.: Kleandros [*Lion-of-men*] of Aegina
wins the pankration at Nemea.

476 B.C.: Theogenes wins the boxing and
Kleandros the pankration at the Isthmian agon.
Theogenes goes on to win the pankration at the
76th Olympiad.

472 B.C.: At the Isthmus, Theogenes wins
boxing and Kallias [*Beautiful*] of Athens pankration.
At the 77th Olympiad Kallias fights into the night
against Theogenes, and is awarded the pankration
win by the Eleans.

471 B.C.: At Nemea, Theogenes wins boxing
and Kallias wins the pankration.

470 B.C.: At the Theseia agon future literary
great Euripides [*Fair-?*] wins the boy's pankration.
At the Isthmus, Theogenes takes the crown in
boxing and Kallias in the pankration. At Pythia
Theogenes does not train for combat sports and
wins the long foot-race, and Kallias wins the
pankration.

469 B.C.: At Nemea Theogenes wins boxing and Kallias is victorious in the pankration.

468 B.C.: At the Isthmus Theogenes wins boxing and Kallias the pankration. Kallias later wins at Olympia.

467 B.C.: At Nemea Theogenes wins boxing and Kallias the pankration.

466 B.C.: At the Isthmus Theogenes wins boxing and Kallias the pankration. Kallias also wins at Delphi.

465 B.C.: At Nemea the boys' pankration is first won by Pytheus [*Snake-lord*] of Argeius; Kallias defeats the men.

464 B.C.: At the Isthmus Pytheus wins the boys' pankration and Kallias defeats the men and retires.

463 B.C.: Thasos surrenders to Athens and Kallias is ostracized from Athens.

461 B.C.: Timodemos [*Honored-of-the-people*] of Athens wins the pankration at Nemea.

460 B.C.: Timodemos wins the pankration at the 80th Olympiad.

458 B.C.: Strepsiades [?] of Thebes wins the pankration at the Isthmus and at Pythia.

456 B.C.: At the 81st Olympiad Dromeus introduces a meat diet and Aristophon of Athens is pankratiast.

452 B.C.: Timanthes of Kleonae is victorious at the 82nd Olympiad. Axionikus writes *The Pankratiast.*

448 B.C.: The boxer Diagoras loses the pankration to his son Damagetus at the 83rd Olympiad.

430s & 420s B.C.: Dorieus [*Spear-lord*], youngest son of Diagoras of Rhodes, dominates the pankration winning 3 Olympic, 4 Delphik, 8 Isthmian and 7 Nemean crowns, some in boxing but most in the pankration. He won 1 Delphik victory without a fight because no one would face him and his most dominant performance was at the 88th Olympiad in 428 which served as a history marker for Thukydides. Timanthes, who had maintained his strength in retirement by continuing to bend a great bow, loses his bow-bending ability after a training lapse, and, in anguish, cremates himself alive in imitation of Herakles.

421 B.C.: Autolykos [*Lone-wolf*] wins the boys' pankration at the PanAthenia.

410s B.C.: In this period the pankration was dominated by the professional soldier Timasithos [*?*] of Thebes, who was perhaps a half-barbarian mercenary. He took 2 Olympic and 3 Delphik crowns.

Noteworthy pankratiasts of the late 5th Century B.C. included Diophanes [*Heavenly -fame*] of Athens, a descendent of Hermolykos, who beat the youths at Isthmus; Androsthenes [*Manly-strength*] of Maenlia who won two Olympic crowns; Antaeus [*Face-to-face-boss*] of Thebes, victor over boys and men at Megara.

Figure 97.

Herakles Boxing

from a Megararian figurine, c.500 B.C.

This figure of Herakles depicts a realistic level of muscular development considering the diet and training methods of the time. Herakles was reputed to have been a short stocky cattle hand native to the region just north of the Megarid, where this piece was fashioned. It is of great interest that he is shown boxing with the hand strap. When considering the early pankration one must keep in mind that strong wrestlers would naturally gravitate to ground and pound tactics. It was not until the Hellenistic period that submission grappling skills among pankratiasts would achieve levels comparable to the ground grappling displayed in modern ultimate fighting venues by Brazillian Jiu-jitsu fighters. The development of submission holds were retarded by the naked and oiled aspect of the fighters.

This figure has the name of the hero carved on his lead left leg. The boxing style depicted is of the archaic school. As this is one of the few pieces of

Classsical boxing art originating outside of Athens, It may safely be assumed that the heavier Dorian boxers of the Greek interior tended to favor this heavy-handed style well into the 5th Century even as the Ionians of Athens, the islands, and the Asian coast evolved boxing styles that kept them at jabbing range. This hard left jab is being posted with an eye to setting up a knockout with the right hand, with the fist configured for a hammering chop with the heel of the hand.

The neck is thick, balance is excellent, and the chin is nicely tucked. A formidable boxer such as this would be a very tough man to beat in the pankration where he would be permitted to kick with his shins, heels and knees, as well as head-butting and elbowing in the standing clinch, from where he could execute a throw or take-down.

Figure 98.
Boxing on the Ground
from an Attic syphos, c.500 B.C.

It appears to the modern eye that these two fighters are boxing out of a referee's position [The kneeling posture used to start the second and third period in modern American folk wrestling]. It is possible that this is a boxing bout, and that the judge to the right is about to thrash these men for clinching. This interpretation is strengthened by the second to the left who is very critical of one or both of the fighter's position.

Whether this is pankration or pugmakhia the action is pretty clear: The bottom fighter is holding his opponent in an open side head-lock with his right while he pushes off the ground with his left and attempts to pull his right leg forward so that he might stand up or roll his opponent. The standing fighter has his man's back and has his left arm wrapped under his chest and is pounding away with a vertical fist uppercut.

It is of particular interest that both of these fighters have their hands strapped for punching. The most entertaining aspect of this scene is somewhat comical; the attitude of disgust and disapproval exhibited by the trainer, who seems to be dismayed by the action.

Figure 99.

Catching the Front-Kick

from a PanAthenaic amphora, c. 490B.C.

The fighter to the right has thrown a lead left kick; probably a foot-jab or front snap kick using the ball of the foot as a striking surface. His opponent has slipped to the inside and cradled the kicking leg with his left as he lifts the leg by pulling up from behind the heel with his right. This is not a simple leg pick-up as indicated by the kicker's standing leg, which is in the correct posture to support a left front kick. The fighter countering the kick with this hold has unwisely bent his head forward and is about to be hammered behind the head and neck. However, this single hammerfist is not likely to keep the kicker off of his back, and he will probably be dumped and mounted shortly. The grappler has the attitude of a patient fighter looking for a submission hold so this should be an interesting ground fight.

Figure 100.

The Round-Kick

From a PanAthenaic amphora c.490 B.C.

The kicker on the right appears to be scoring to his opponent's thigh with a powerful round-kick thrown either from a left lead, or, for more power, from a right lead. The most interesting aspect of this scene is the response of the fighter on the left, who appears to be countering by slipping his left arm under the kicker's knee and grasping the extended foot with his rear right hand. This counter seems to be the opening sequence for the leg lift counter to the front kick depicted in Figure 99.

This fact begs the question: were Figures 100 and 99 reverse sides of the same vase representing two phases of the same fight? If so than Figure 100 is the initial exchange with 99 being the second phase of a fight destined to go to the ground. This interpretation can be supported by all of the postures in the two scenes, even those of the judge. If such is the case, than what the author has interpreted as a spent front kick in Figure 99 would actually be the spent round kick from Figure 100 having been turned after the clinch. If these figures do not represent a sequence than we have evidence for a standard grappling counter to a kick which was generalized enough to be effective against at least two types of kick.

This figure and the preceding one taken together make a fascinating study unfortunately rendered murky by the poor state of the existing copies of this piece.

Figure 101.

Gouging on the Ground

from an Attic cup c.480B.C.

The fighter on the right has some leg-to-leg control but is in a bad spot as his opponent is covering his mouth and punching him to the solar plexus with vertical upper cuts. In desperation he has begun to gouge his tormentor's right eye with both thumbs. For this the judge is thrashing him with his forked rod of willow—which must have absolutely hurt like hell. Such rod strokes would cause deep narrow welts and produce some bleeding.

It seems that the only penalty for such a blatant foul is the actual beating with the rod until the rule-breaker desists. Disqualification for fouling was probably reserved for those who defeated an adversary as a result of unsanctioned tactics.

Figure 102.

The Fish-Hook

from an Attic cup c.480B.C.

      The uppermost pankratiast is fish-hooking the prone fighter's mouth by tearing the cheek with his left thumb as he hammers away with his right fist. The fish-hook seems to have been used to throw the man down as his feet are still in the air. This has been a quickly executed technique as the judge is still using his rod to keep the fighters from stepping off the dug-up, and has not yet noticed the fish-hook. This fight is over and might well represent one of those times when a victorious fighter would be disqualified for winning by a foul. If this were a preliminary round at an agon the fish-hooker would be prevented from advancing. If this were the final bout of an agon then the prize would be dedicated to the god or hero of the agon.

      The figure to the right is interesting. Might this be a female breaking taboo by viewing this contest?

Figure 103.

Positioning for the Kick

from an Attic vase 430B.C.

Gardiner misinterpreted this piece as representing wrestlers or pankratiasts about to engage in a clinch. However, these postures have obvious parallels with modern oriental boxing, which was little known and less understood in Gardiner's day. The posture of the fighter on the left is evocative of Chinese boxing. The fighter on the right seems to be positioning for a left foot jab and or a back leg round kick in a style more similar to Thai boxing. Notice both fighters are observing good boxing form from an orthodox [left-lead] stance with hands held high. The high open-hand guard suggests an advanced level of kick-boxing expertise, and the possibility that low-line kicks would be dealt with by a defending foot, shin or knee technique.

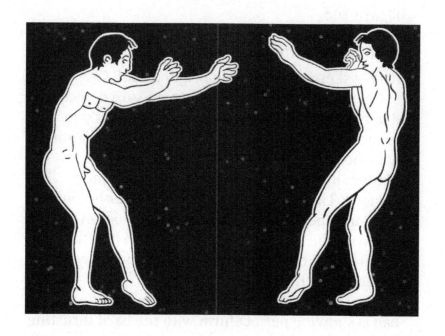

Figure 104.

Dwarves Kicking the Heavy Bag

from a sketch of uncertain origin c.420B.C.

Why the athletes in this scene are depicted as dwarves is unclear. However, at about this date—at least in Athens, where this piece may or may not have been drawn—the caricaturing of prize-fighters had become a popular form of minor comedy. The dwarf to the left is a trainer holding what may be a victory palm as a reminder of the honors to be won through training. On his stomach are etched 5 or 6 obscured letters which may spell his name or title.

The dwarf pankratiast working the heavy bag is showing perfect form with the hard thrusting foot jab. He is demonstrating with his hand form all of the tools necessary to prevail in the all-power-thing. His extended lead hand is positioned to ward against the knee grab; to fire a finger jab to the eyes, solar plexus or throat; or simply push off to make room or sprawl on an opponent who has gotten too close. His rear hand is chambered for a plunging straight right which would develop great force if landed with the hard left step that would follow a lead left kick-push combination. His posture is similar to, but more efficient than, that depicted by the fighter on the left in Figure 94.

The heavy bag may have been filled with sand, barley, beans, saw-dust or whatever blend of fill was preferred at the time. [In late antiquity the heavy bag was used by the pankratiast exclusively

174

and was filled with sand.] The bag itself is a complete pig skin hung by its tail. Pig skin—which is used in modern times to cover the American footballs—would be very rough on the hands, particularly the knuckles. Therefore such a bag was probably used exclusively for practicing kicking, clinching, and open-hand blows. An all-power-fighter would hone his punching skills primarily on the light bag or dummy preferred by boxers.

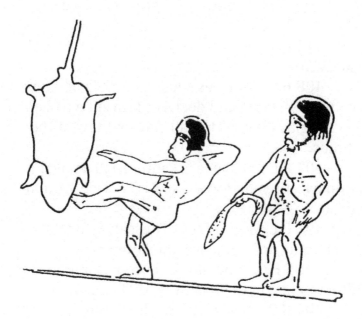

Giants of the Classical Pankration: 411 to 365 B.C.

"The statue on the high pedestal is the work of Lysippus, and represents the tallest of men except those known as heroes and other immortals who may have existed before the heroes. But this man, Polydamas [*Many-subduer*] the son of Nikias of Skotussa, is the tallest man of the mortal age."
-Pausanias, *Description of Greece*

411 B.C.: Dorieus leads Rhodes in a revolt against Athens.

408 B.C.: Dorieus seconds for his nephews in boxing at Olympia and declares himself a citizen of Thurii. Agias [?] wins the all-power-thing at the Isthmus.

407 B.C.: Dorieus is captured in a naval action by Athenian forces, and is set free without ransom.

406 B.C.: Agias [?] of Thessaly wins the all-power-thing at Delphi and the Isthmus.

c.405 B.C.: Polydamas becomes famous for bull-wrestling in the pastures of Thessaly.

404 B.C.: Agias wins at the Isthmus. Polydamas wins the all-power-thing at Olympia, probably stopping Agias, and shows off for the crowd by holding back a racing chariot. He then journeys to Mount Olympus and kills a lion with his bare hands in his mania to emulate Herakles. The 30-year long Peloponnesian war finally ends with the defeat of Athens by Sparta.

403 B.C.: Timasithos serves as a mercenary in a Spartan supported coup in Athens, putting The Thirty Tyrants in power, and is later executed by the Athenians after the fall of the Thirty.

402 B.C.: Polydamas journeys to Persian Susa and fights the Three Immortals before King Dareius. Agias stops Promakhus in the all-power-thing at the Isthmus and again at Delphi.

401 B.C.: Cyrus, a claimant to the Persian throne, leads an army against Darius at Cunaxa, where he is killed. Cyrus' Greek mercenaries retire in good order, elect Xenophon of Athens as their leader, and conduct a fighting withdraw through the mountains of Armenia. Polydamas returns to Greece where Promakhus has just won the pankration at Nemea.

400 B.C.: Agias is victorious at the Isthmus in the spring. At about the same time Xenophon's army reaches Trapezus on the Black Sea and elects to stage an agon. This agon was contrary to the Olympic model: with barbarian slaves competing and common women [prostitutes] watching. A Spartan murderer named Drakontius was elected agonios. He marked off the dug-up for wrestling, boxing and pankration on the rocky overgrown mountainside, and declared that getting thrown would be unusually painful. Although there is no record of the winners of the wrestling and pankration it seems that the sleazy Thessalian Boskius won the boxing, and that the competition was made fiercer than usual due to the prostitutes' encouragement.

In late summer, Agias fails to stop Polydamas and Promakhus at Olympia. Promakhus emerged victorious in the final bout against Polydamas. Promakhus' success is attributed to the sage advice of his trainer who talked the young contender out of having sex with his beautiful and insistent young girlfriend while preparing for the 95th Olympiad.

399 B.C.: Promakhus wins the Nemean pankration. The death of Sokrates at Athens.

388 B.C.: Promakhus wins the Isthmian pankration and Agias wins the Pythian pankration.

397 B.C.: Promakhus wins the Nemean all-power-thing.

396 B.C.: Promakhus wins the Isthmian pankration and Agias finally wins the crown at Olympia.

395 B.C.: Rhodes revolts against Sparta. Dorieus is captured and executed by the Spartans.

394 B.C.: An eclipse of the sun was noted, an event thought to show divine displeasure. The powerful commercial city of Korinth, host of the Isthmian games, goes to war with Pellene, the small home-town of Promakhus. The small army of Pellene advances on Korinth, with the Olympian Promakhus [*Front-line-fighter*] in the first rank. He becomes the hero of his people at the battle of Korinth, and is credited with killing a vast number of the enemy. The importance of having such an athlete in the front ranks of a hoplite army was attested to by the ancient Spartan practice of stationing the Olympic champions with the King in battle. Such importance was placed on having the

best, and best armed, [Promakhus would have been both] hoplites in the front rank that this guaranteed a weaker second rank. Once a dominant fighter like Promakhus [who would have been like an NFL linebacker on a high school football field] dispatched the man in front of him, it would have been successively less difficult for him to bowl over the rear ranks, and devastating to the enemy formation if he turned right after penetrating the ranks. Such a rigid infantry formation is mechanically and psychologically brittle and highly vulnerable to such stress.

"So when his soldiers saw them white because they never stripped their bodies under the sun, and fat and lazy through constant riding in carts, they believed that the war would be like a battle against women."
   -Xenophon, on the campaign of Agisilaus against the Persians, from the *Scripta Minora*

   384 B.C.: Hippas of Elis has his Olympic register set up by the Olympian Paraballon.
   380 B.C.: At the 100th Olympiad Isokrates distributes his *Panegyric* and Astyanax [*Town-chief*] of Miletus wins the all-power-thing. The duties of the Pythian officials are inscribed at Delphi.
   370s B.C.: Anaxippus writes *The Thunderbolt*, featuring critical depictions of combat athletes. Plato begins writing his social commentaries. In Athens a social group emerges known as the Lakonizers, who emulated

conservative Spartan traditions: wearing short cloaks and leather belts and practicing combat sports. These men were noted boxers and grapplers with the deformed ears of the prize-fighter.

"He has a fierce look and arching eye-brows, his shoulders are brawny, and he shows a sturdy thigh."

-Alkiphron, on a dangerous man, from his *Letters*

376 B.C.: At the 101st Olympiad Antiokhus wins the pentathlon and Astyanax wins the pankration.

375 B.C.: Antiokhus of Lepreus wins the pentathlon at the Nemean agon.

373 B.C.: The site of the Pythian agon at the sanctuary of Apollo at Delphi is severely damaged by an earthquake. Antiokhus wins the pentathlon at Nemea again.

372 B.C.: At the 102nd Olympiad Antiokhus of Lepreus wins the pentathlon and then goes on to win the all-power-thing, probably defeating Astyanax in the final bout. Antiokhus, hailing from the town of Lepreus, which had produced generations of Olympic fist-fighting champions, was probably an elite boxer.

371 B.C.: Skotussa, home of Polydamas, is wiped out through an act of treachery by Jason, Tyrant of Pherae. At the battle of Leuktra the Spartan King and his bodyguard of elite athletes are

killed to a man when they are defeated by the 50-man-deep phalanx of Theban hoplites under Epimondas. Antiokhus is sent by the towns of Arkadia as an ambassador to the Persian king.

370 B.C.: While on the run from Jason, who has become master of Thessaly, Polydamas and his surviving friends hide out in a grotto to drink wine. Possibly due to after-shocks from the quake of 373 and the drinking songs of the refugees, the walls and ceiling of the grotto began to collapse. As his friends fled the cave-in, Polydamas stayed behind and died while attempting to hold back the collapsing mountainside. His friends in Thessaly thought him a hero, while philosophers thought him an idiot. Diophanes [*Heavenly-fame*] II wins the youth pankration at the Isthmian agon.

While Jason was planning his invasion of Persia, a gymnasiarkh named Taxillus petitioned him for permission to discipline some young gym rats who had worked him over. Jason permitted him to fine them 300 drakhmas or ten strokes of the rod each. Later that year, when Jason was presiding over the Pythian agon, he was assassinated by the angry young men that had beaten, and been punished by, Taxillus.

360s B.C.: Turmoil in the region of Olympia continues and pankratiasts start to develop a reputation as parasites [party-crashers, and personal bodyguards of Tyrants]. Thyphilus writes *The All-power-fighter*.

"He was a man fierce of aspect, cruel, and terribly gluttonous."
                    -Atheneas on Lythersas of Phrygia

368 B.C.: At the 103rd Olympiad the judges are increased from 10 to 12 and Astyanax wins the pankration for the third time. If not for Antiokhus he would have been the only 4-time Olympic pankratiast.

367 B.C.: Astyanax, in the role of an ambassador, is invited to dine with the Persian governor Ariobarzanes. On a dare, Astyanax ate all the food that had been prepared for six men. To demonstrate his strength he broke off a bronze lentil-shaped ornament from a couch, which he bent and then straightened with the strength of his hands alone.

366 B.C.: Ariobarzanes revolts from Persian rule. Isokrates writes *Arkhidamas*.

365 B.C.: The Arkadians invade Elis and conquer Olympia. Antiokhus may well have been among the soldiers who seized the scene of his double victory seven years earlier.

Summary: From 411 to 365 B.C. all six of the dominant all-power-fighters served as political, military or diplomatic leaders. It is also notable that lesser pankratiasts of this period were becoming notorious for throwing their weight around on the domestic political scene. They were simply aping their betters.

Figure 105.
Agias of Thessaly, c. 400 B.C.
From a 4th Century marble copy of the 5th Century
bronze statue by Lysippus

    Sculpted and raised to honor his single
Olympic victory in the pankration two generations
after the fact, the figure of Agias presents us with
the physique of the prime pankration contenders
that would have faced such greats as Polydamas
and Promokhus in the second round at Olympia.
His build differs little from the famous sculptures of
Polyklitus [the *Spear-bearer* and *Crown-wearer*]
with the exception that Agias appears to have the
heavier rounded shoulders of the boxer. At between
5' 10" and 6' in height, Agias possessed the build of
a modern middle-weight MMA fighter.

    The statue was commissioned by Agias'
grandson, Daokhus II, co-ruler of Thessaly.
Although he was victorious three times at Delphi
and five times at the Isthmus, he only won one
crown at Olympia and failed to win or enter at
Nemea. His record and the date of his grandson's
dedication clearly indicate that he was a
contemporary of Polydamas and Promakhus, and
that he failed to best them at Olympia. He did,
however, have a better overall record and it is likely
that he met Promakhus often, losing to him at
Nemea [in Promokhus' homeland], splitting at the
Isthmus [on sleazy neutral ground], and besting
him at Delphi [in Agias' homeland]. As for
Polydamas, the men of Thessaly claimed that he

was never beaten, and their statues were carved by the same hand and possibly commissioned by the same man. It appears that Polydamas only competed at Olympia, and spent the balance of his *agonistic* energy on his crazed quest to emulate Herakles.

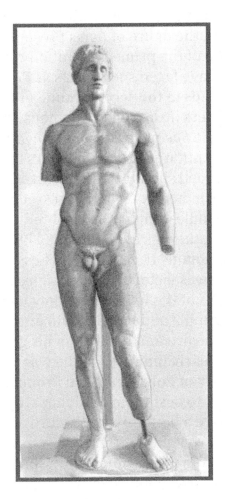

Figure 106
The Face of Polydamas
Based on a marble head by Lysippos c.335 B.C.

Below is the caption for an action illustration featurimg Polydamas that was discarded as too time consuming for an interior piece during our final planning session in 2005.

Having been invited by Darieus, King of Kings, ruler of the vast Persian Empire, to journey into the highlands of present day Iran to present himself, Polydamas challenged three opponents at once. These three men were the best of the King's personal body guard of 10,000 "Immortals", so named because the number was always kept at 10,000 through replacements. These soldiers had experience fighting alongside and against Greek heavy infantry and were regarded as tough, brave and strong. However, the Persians were a horse culture with no boxing tradition. They were, as the men of Iran are today, renowned wrestlers. Their specific discipline would have been similar to modern Mongolian or Turkish wrestling, being a stand-up throwing art utilizing jacket, belt and pants holds.

Polydamas' massive size and freakish strength, augmented by his striking ability made this 3 on 1 bout a 1 on 3 slaughter. It is unknown what techniques Polydamas employed to defeat the three soldiers, who all died as a result of their injuries.

The action rendered in this reconstruction is based on written accounts of the fighting methods of Jeremiah Johnson, a 1830s mountain man who single-handedly fought a war against the Crow Nation and killed 50 Crow warriors. Many of his kills were gained by kicking his much smaller Amerindian adversaries in the chest, causing heart failure, and lung collapse and perforation. Polydamas may have used a kick to dispatch his closest antagonist.

The course of the bout is envisioned as a piece-meal destruction by Polydamas of each Persian in succession as he ignores the others. This is precisely the tactic used by unarmed modern compulsive fighters to attack and destroy groups of 2 to 5 antagonists in American street encounters. As these were athletic warriors wearing beards and cloths and compelled to attack aggressively before their master the King, it is likely that Polydamas had an easy time of it as his enemies stepped forward to be held and punched.

The most aggressive Persian lays dead from a massive chest trauma as his two comrades attempt to grapple with the naked oiled giant who holds the one who has a access to his groin by the beard with his left hand as he hammers the doomed warrior's collar bone, upper spine, and base of the skull with his brick-sized fist. The third Persian may fall victim to some variation on this theme. As his clinch will no doubt be sunk deep around the waist Polydamas could elbow, knee and push his way to outer range where he could show off for the King with his feet and fists.

All-in-all this would be as competitive as [and also socially analogous to] the *Ultimate Fighting Challenge Heavyweight Champion* taking on three unarmed security guards at the Mall of America. The author envisions Polydamas as physically similar to MMA fighter Semmy Shilt.

Late Classical Pankratiasts: 364 to 325 B.C.

"Take care that in guarding Heaven you don't lose Earth."
    -Demades, on the deification of Alexander

364 B.C.: The Arkadians hold the 104th Olympiad, where they battle in the sacred precinct against a force of Eleans, who, after reclaiming the sanctuary, count the 104th as an anoOlympiad. Sostratus [*The-warrior*] of Sikyon, wins the all-power-thing, and becomes known as Akrokheirsites [*High-hander*], and becomes famous for breaking his opponents' fingers.

363 B.C.: Sostratus is victorious in the Nemean pankration. Thebes commits the Orkhomenian genocide.

362 B.C.: Sostratus wins the pankration at the Isthmus and Delphi. The Thebans lose hegamony with their defeat at the battle of Mantinea. The rebellious Ariobarzanes is defeated and crucified by the Persians.

361 B.C.: Sostratus wins the all-power-thing at Nemea.

360 B.C.: A colossal gym is built at Delphi. Sostratus wins at the Isthmus and at Olympia.

359 B.C.: Sostratus is victorious at the Nemean agon.

358 B.C.: Sostratus wins at the Isthmus, at the same agon where Diogenes Kynikos [*The Dog*] gives a speech featuring the following excerpt, "The toughest and hardest to defeat, who no Greek can stare down. Not those athletes who run or wrestle or jump or those who box or throw the javelin or stone, but those who challenge a man with words."

After this well-received speech The Dog, squatted and relieved his bowels before the stunned crowd!

357 B.C.: Sostratus is victorious at Nemea.

356 B.C.: At the 106th Olympiad Philip of Makedon wins the horse race [Alexander is born to Philip and Olympius in this year.]; and Sostratus and Khaereas sweep the fist and all-power combats.

355 B.C.: Diogenes founds the philosophy of Cynicism. Sostratus is victorious at Nemea.

354 B.C.: Sostratus wins his last all-power-thing at the Isthmus. His record will stand for 400 years.

353 B.C.: Athens commits the genocide of Sestus.

c.350 B.C.: Athletes journeying to compete at Athens are granted special amenities if they bring with them a measure of grain to sell to Athens, a tradition perhaps 100 years old. Victors in the all-power-thing at the PanAthenic agon are awarded the following prizes: boys' 1st place = 40 jugs of olive oil [$16,000]; boys' second place = 8 jugs [$3,200]; youths' 1st place = 50 jugs [$20,000]; youths' 2nd place = 10 jugs [$4,000]; mens' 1st place = 80 jugs [$32,000]; mens' 2nd place = 16 jugs [$6,500]. The vast majority of the prize-fighting artwork from the 6th, 5th, and 4th Centuries B.C. that have survived into modern times consists of prize amphora. Yet the total number of surviving jugs are only a fraction of those that might be awarded at a single *agon*. The winner of the Athenian pankration received 80 works of art painted with scenes of combat and filled with a substance as valuable as cash and also useful for his diet and training.

340s B.C.: Extensive construction at Olympia: stadium renovation; construction of Theokoleum and Leonidaeum. After the death and cremation of Astyanax his bones are too massive to fit in the funeral urn. Antiphanes [*Against-fame*] wins the boy's pankration at the Panathenaic agon.

342 B.C.: At the 61st Pythiad Iolades [?] of Thebes wins the first boys' *pankration* at Delphi.

338 B.C.: Lysippus sculpts the likenesses of Agias and Polydamas and raises them in the Altis at Olympia.

336 B.C.: At the 111th Olympiad, Dioxippos [*Heavenly-reaper*] wins the pankration, he is seconded by his sparring partner Euphraios [*Fair-?*] who is said to be the strongest man in Hellas; Alexander raises the statues of his family next to the statue of Theogenes; and Aristotle updates the Olympic Register.

334 B.C.: Dioxippos joins Alexander in his invasion of the Persian Empire. Xenarkes [*Stranger's-aid*] of Stratus wins the all-power-thing at the Isthmus and at Delphi.

333 B.C.: Alexander is victorious at the Battle of Issus. Xenarkes wins the Nemean pankration.

332 B.C.: At the 112th Olympiad Xenarkes wins the pankration.

331 B.C.: The foundation of Alexandria in Egypt and the Battle of Gaugamela are celebrated with agons.

330 B.C.: Alexander conquers Persia. The building of the *Metroon* at Olympia.

329-326 B.C.: Alexander conquers at least 10 tribal nations and commits numerous genocides. Border settlements with athletic facilities are founded and populated by discharged Greek mercenaries.

325 B.C.: Alexander's army slaughters the Kshatriyas in India and his bodyguard Koragus challenges Dioxippos to a duel at a party. Kragus comes to the duel the following morning, armored and armed with javelin, lance, shield and sword. Dioxippos fought naked and armed with a club in honor of Herakles. Dioxippos dodged the javelin, knocked the lance aside, and put Koragus down, allowing him to live. This monomakhia was fought before the entire army. To soothe Makedonian pride Alexander's henchmen have Dioxippos killed and forge a suicide letter.

Figure 107.

The Fingerer

at the 106th Olympiad of 356 B.C.
artist's conception

Sostratus [*The-warrior*] Akrokheirsites [*High-hander*] of Sikyon gains victory in the all-power-thing against a prime Athenian fighter, who signals defeat with his raised right finger as Sostratus utilizes his freakishly strong grip to bend back the man's fingers for a submission via small-joint manipulation, a tactic which is banned in modern MMA.

Sostratus' stature is unknown, but the fact that he relied on finger holds to secure victory suggests that he lacked the body mass for dominant ground work or the long reach required to dominate the action at kicking and punching range. His sir name, Akrokheirsites, is more likely to suggest the ability to master the art of high-handedness at close range—perhaps by trapping—than the common misinterpretation that he was a crude finger-breaker. Crude doesn't get it done consistently in MMA. However, the ability to consistently target the hands of powerful grapplers and light-handed boxers, who may well have been younger and larger than himself, suggests four dynamics that might have explained Sostratus' dominance: highly attuned tactile sensitivity; disproportionately strong hands and forearms; a singularly ruthless nature which must have transfixed his opponents with dread; and a true mixed-martial arts approach to training... boxing the grapplers, grappling the boxers, and punishing the all-round fighters with cruel finger holds.

In a small polis like Sikyon it is likely that all the combat athletes trained together out of the same palaestra. The stable of Sikyonian fighters no doubt looked to Sostratus as their mentor, as he was the most dominant athlete of the day. It is noteworthy that Sostratus travelled to sacred *agons* on at least two occassions with Khaereas who won two Olympic crowns, probably with Sostratus serving as his trainer. It is likely, that at this date, while the aging Sostratus was defending the Olympic dug-up, which had become his "turf", that he would have been seconded by Khaereas, who had taken the crown for the fist just hours ago, and is pictured in the background squatting on his haunches and reminding his team mate to keep his shoulders hunched and his chin tucked, necessary precautions for a known finger-breaker to avoid getting a thumb or finger spear in the eyes.

The All-Power-Thing at Landbridge: 358 B.C.

The guardians of the contest truce were everywhere evident among the stalls, tents and training digs. The heavy-armed-men of Tower-hill in their finery, barbarian sentries in their animal hides, and heralds and pipers accompanied the rod-bearers on their rounds. The elderly trainer acknowledged the priests of the Earth-shaker and the Escort-of-souls, and turned to his fighter, "Contest truces were sacred in my day. Now the prize-givers must hire killers to protect the very contest, and these umpires—holy men you would think—remind me of the bruisers that guard our whorehouses back in Thought."

The young man's response reflected his own curiosity more than his master's opinion, "Will we remain in camp? Or will we visit the city?"

The old man pointed his oft broken finger at the high-walled city, "That? That den of whore-mongers? No fighter of mine so much as drinks the water there! Any youth with enough juice left in his balls to ask that question hasn't been sparring enough. Besides, there is work for you before the contest. The goatherd king from up north aspires to culture, so he has sent some of his crude brawlers to train for the contest. You will be my teaching rod. So think only of them and the prize-seekers that will oppose you in your age class, and I'll get you a nice scented priestess after contest-day."

The two picked their way through the training digs, eye-balling their rivals, and came to a small circle of military tents guarded by some foul-smelling barbarian missile men with faces painted black and wolf-hides over their shoulders. The youth could not contain himself after sighting his rivals among the digs, "Bodytaker, may I fight as a man? I'm better than the youths here by far..."

The elder cut him off sharply, "Be glad these rich bastards are allowing a youth class; a big draw it is—tyrants hunting prospects for Thunder-chief's olive crown. You're not ready for the best men just yet. I'll enter you as a youth if I have to shave the hair off your ass to prove it! No more questions Reaper. Listen in while I deal with these murderers. You'll have to deal with their kind after I've descended to the halls of dust."

The two were barred from nearing the tents by the evil-smelling missile-men who barked at one another like dogs working a flock of sheep. After a brief but tense moment, a short muscular man in armor emerged from the central tent and greeted the old man in a harsh accent, "You are Bodytaker of Thought, come to train my men?"

"Yes strategist, along with Reaper, my best youth."

The cruel man looked upon Bodytaker, old and bent, but still tall, with scorn, "Why has he chosen you? I would have preferred a man of Rope or Grassland. Why should my men heed your word; with one foot already in your tomb?"

Reaper grew angry and wanted to kick this killer's teeth into the sand. However, his master's tone remained even, one might even say soothing, "Because, son, your master has decided for you. Perhaps he has decided to honor this broken old man because we shared a cell at Sevengate; or perhaps because I was All-Thought Victor six years running, and lost this contest as many times. Perhaps this is my redemption."

The elder then put a fatherly hand on the Strategist's shoulder and pointed to his four burly shield-fighters, "You fellows, you will be training to fight The Warrior, also known as High-hander. He has known only victory. He will circle you and chop you down with kicks. If you manage to get him to the clinch he will snap your fingers like straw and stomp your teeth into the earth.

We will train to beat him though, because there would be no greater honor to bring back to your king. This youth here, is my prize disciple. He is nearly a master at body-circling. You men will begin sparring with him immediately. He fights to stay on his feet. You must fight to take your man down. You all will benefit from this practice equally. Chance of victory is slim. But if victopry comes it will be wonderful boys, wonderful!
On contest-day we go against The Warrior, and against all those others that seek him as well. But he, the finger-breaker, he is your prey. And, remember this, if one of you is fortunate enough to

take him into the dirt, than be sure to listen to that crazed old man screaming instructions, because that will be me, in my joy."

Figure 108.

Taking Down the Kicker

from PanAthenaic amphora from Eretria, 360/59 B.C.

These all-power-fighters appear to be kickboxers as they both have their hands strapped. It seems that the fighter on the left has side-stepped a back-leg front kick, caught the heel of the passed leg—which appears to be the common Greek counter to the spent kick—and has put his man down simply by grabbing the hair with his fingers and pushing on the forehad with his palm. The fallen fighter still appears to be trying to pry off the offending hand with his own. [An alternative reading of the head grab would be a palm thrust which has gotten through the fallen fighter's high guard. The author prefers the static reading only because it is so hard to slip a palm strike between two guarding hands.]

Victory seems assured for the standing fighter, who's appearance is lost due to damage to the art. It appears that this is the record of some sacred triumph supposed to be sanctioned by the gods, for Athena stands to the left looking on with the palm of victory ready to bestow on the victor, and the pale-skinned image of Nike [*Winged-victory*] is hovering over the dominant fighter with her alabaster arms outstretched towards his head, upon which she is no doubt placing a crown of victory.

One is left to wonder whether the officials of some agons did not employ costumed women to play the parts of Athena and Nike? There is the precedence of such use of a costumed woman in Archaic Athens for political intrigue [Herodotus 1.60]

Figure 109.

Hammering in the Clinch

from a PanAthenaic amphora, 332 B.C.

The fighter on the right appears to be a wrestler poorly schooled in all-power-fighting who has shot in for a waist tackle. His opponent has under hooked his throat with his lead left forearm and the wrestler has instantly fixated on this unsecured hold by seizing the stand-up fighters forearm. By grappling in such a naive manner against a more experienced fighter, he has given up the back of his head and neck to the legal hammer blows of his opponent, who will surely win by knock out.

To the right, the judge stands by with the rod of discipline and crown of victory, while a second, or possibly the next opponent for the winner of this bout, stands off to the left.

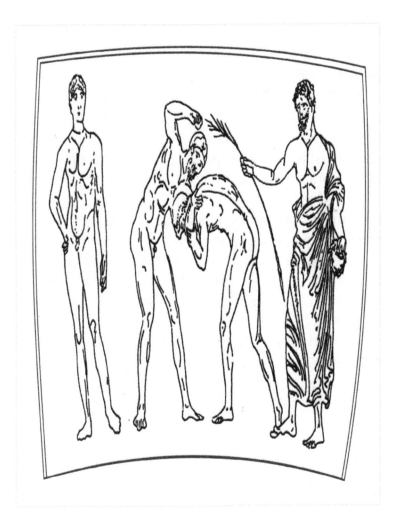

An Analysis of Pankration Techniques in Art & Literature: 648 to 325 B.C.

Scenes: 34
Techniques: 97
Kicks: 13
Punches: 39
Elbows: 1
Gouges: 6
Two-handed hold: 17
One-handed Hold: 18
Head-butts: 2
Knees: 1
Median techniques depicted per scene: 2.9

A Stylistic Summary of Early Pankration to 325 B.C.

The evolution of pankration archetypes can be broken into three distinct phases:

1. From 648 to 500 B.C. all-power-fighting was dominated by well-rounded grapplers.

2. From 500 to 410 B.C. all-power-fighting was dominated by boxers from the islands of Thasos, Aegina and Rhodes, although specialized ground-grapplers trained in Athens and Thebes remained a huge threat. The dominance of boxers during this period is related to the simultaneous emergence of high-handedness as a winning approach to boxing and as a stalling strategy in wrestling.

3. From 410 to 325 B.C. true mixed-martial arts practitioners of all-power-fighting emerged from schools out of small mainland towns. As boxing became more specialized and oriented toward power hitting it ceased to be the basis for a dominant pankration style.

The dominant style throughout the entire period seems to be the aggressive "ground-and-pound" school of hybrid boxing as opposed to the defensive "sprawl-and-brawl" school of hybrid boxing. However, the record is punctuated by the appearance of giants such as Lygdamas and Polydamas who could win on pure genetics, and master grapplers like Melisias and Kallias of Athens. When considering the style most respected by practitioners and spectators, one must consider that the high point of all ancient combat sports was considered by many ancient scholars to be the tenacious submission grappling of Arrikhion, and that the most feared of all pankratiasts were Dorieus the boxer and Sostratus the finger-bender.

Even at these early dates the ancient Greek pankration had every stylistic angle and more drama and brutality than the sport of modern MMA, which is just reaching adolescence in the second decade of the 21st Century. In conclusion, if anything negative can be said about the earliest all-power-fighters it is that they don't seem to have been very effective kickers.

The Cultural Context of Archaic & Classical Pankration

Overall, the social standing of pankration was split into three functions. First and foremost was the concept of a sport that would give the spectators and competitors a vision of heroic dominance.

On the social level the entire game seems to have been an exercise in mythic yearning to generate contemporary legends that would rival and validate the legendary figure of manliness that meant so much to the spirit of Greek enterprise, Herakles, who would one day become the patron god of business. There was something about the image of Herakles that the ancients wanted desperately to nurture in their cruel agonizing way; perhaps so that they could believe that the legends were true, or simply so that they could see the birth of a legend before their eyes.

On the military level the pankration consistently produced effective battlefield leaders in the heavy ranks: Phrynon, general of Athens; Hermolykos, hero of Athens; Lygdamas, a mercenary captain of Naxos who fought for Athenian exiles; Dorieus, admiral of Rhodes; Timasithos, mercenary captain of Thebes; Promakhus, point-man of Pellene; Antiokhus, ambassador and warrior of Lepreus; and Dioxiphos of Athens, hero of the Greeks in India. The pankration required calculated application of diverse combat skills under extreme stress while in enemy contact. This most demanding form of combat seemed well suited for developing the characteristics required of battlefield leaders in an age when generals got their hands bloody.

Finally, the all-power-thing and its extreme practitioners provided the professional thinkers of the day with a wonderful metaphor for discussion, even as the sport provided outrageous characters for the poets and comics. The pankration was to the ancient Greek military institutions what the military academies of West Point and Annapolis are to the modern U.S. Army and U.S. Navy: an institution primarily attuned to the development of an adaptable martial character among potential leaders.

Figure 110.

Centaur and Lapith

Metope from the Partheneon at Athens, c. 440 B.C.

The ninety-two battle scenes carved on the greatest building of Classical Hellas depicted mythic and contemporary conflicts in brutal detail. These were among the earliest decorations to be carved on a building.

This piece, from the median point of our inquiry, utilizes highly evolved practical unarmed fighting techniques to illustrate a mythic battle between savagery and civilization. The Centaur represents the unsettled nomad who occasionally threatened Greece. His opponent, the Lapith, represents the young man of excellence defending his homeland and kinsmen.

The Lapith has kneed the rearing man-horse, who has countered by tying up the kneeing leg with his forelegs and shooting out his left hand for the choke. Instead of attempting to break the choke, the Lapith is scoring with a hyper-pronated overhand right [a corkscrew punch] to the temple. The fight seems to hang very much in the balance, with both fighters chambered for a knockout punch; the centaur with a hammer-fist, and the Lapith with a long left uppercut.

This combat achieves a perfect synergy between the mythic foundations and metaphoric importance of the all-power-thing, and the actual combative excellence in unarmed contests that marked the Classical all-power-fighters as some of the most accomplished martial artists in human history.

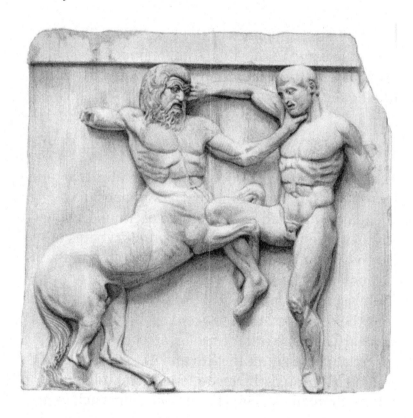

The Fate of Athletics after Alexander

"...and Sophanes of Dekelea, who killed,
when he came to the aid of the Aeginetans,
Eurybates [*Broad-step*] the Argive, who had won
the five-exercises at the Nemean agon."
-Pausanias, *Description of Greece*

The passage above commemorates two fallen
war heroes, the monomakhaist Sophanes of
Dekelea, who died in the service of Athens against
the Thrakians, and the pentathlete Eurybates of
Argos, who died in the service of Aegina against the
Athenians. These events [c.465 B.C.] were not the
only occasions in Classical times when pentathletes
or other combat athletes acted as individual
military allies to other Greek states. It was common
practice throughout the 5th and 4th centuries B.C.
for such famous athletes to lend their weight to
often doomed causes. The reasons why such men
became military adventurers willing to take up the
cause of another people must be partially due to
their risk-taking nature; a characteristic shared by

all top-level combat athletes. Another likely cause is the lure of wealth through mercenary service. Finally, however, the reason for certain famous athletes lending such military services may well be based on the contacts they had made on the athletic circuit. Perhaps Eurybates' trainer was an Aeginetan? Perhaps Timasithieos, the Theban pankratiast and mercenary captain, had developed personal ties to certain high-ranking Athenians who were avid pankration practitioners, and that some such athletic/political connection led to his being recruited to support the coup of the Thirty Tyrants in 403 B.C.?

Despite the drastic change in military systems and geopolitics in the years following the death of Alexander the Great, combat athletes continued to play a prominent role in small-scale warfare in the Greek home country. The formation of political leagues by the small city-states in the age of Alexander's successors marked a return to small-scale battles and skirmishes where captains gained fame and boosted troop morale by slaying their enemy counter-part in monomakhia. The most famous of these generals who dueled was Philopeomen, General of the Akheaen League from 222 to 183 B.C. Although, as his name suggests, he loved war and scorned athletics, he was a great natural athlete, who, it was said, could have won fame in the panHellenik agons had he competed.

There were two figures, both pentathletes, who had distinguished military careers during this period. In both cases, there initial appointment to command seems to have been at least partially based on their athletic achievements. These men were Gorgus [*Fierce*] of Messene, and Timon [*Honored*] of Elis.

Gorgus, son of Eukletus, was an Olympic victor in the pentathlon in the mid 200s B.C., and went on to hold a military command, for the resurrected city-state of Messene, which was no longer under Spartan rule.

Timon of Elis had one of the most distinguished pentathlon careers in history. As such he represented the best of the Elean officer corp, for the people of Elis did select their cavalry commanders—and they were known for having a good cavalry force—from amongst their pentathletes. Of the 29 panHellenik pentathlon champions sited by Pausanias 11 of them were Eleans.

After victories at Olympia, Pythia and Nemea, Timon shuned the Isthmiad in honor of Moline's curse. He then joined the Aetolians in their war against the Thessalians, and distinguished himself to such a degree [c.285 B.C.] that he was granted command of the garrison of Naupaktus. Timon's statue is situated in the Altis next to the personification of Hellas [*Greece*] and of Elis. These deities are depicted crowning the Makedonian warrior-kings Antigonus and Demetrius who fought wars in alliance with Elis and other small Greek states against the invading Gauls who sacked Delphi, and the successors of Alexander in Asia and

Africa: Seleukus and Ptolemy. Timon apparently served Elis and her allies in these wars that were fought between 290 and 270 B.C.

As Philopeomen's refusal to enter athletic agons and his resignation from his post as cavalry commander in favor of infantry duty, predicted, the new revolution in infantry combat and siege warfare begun in 4th Century Makedonia and now rampant in Italy, would push athletes and their arts off of the battlefield and training ground where they were born, and into the rarified arena of elite cultural ritual that was the agon of late antiquity, and the reeking maniacal stew of mass entertainment that was the Roman arena. The best prize-fighters in history were yet to be born; but they would be celebrities, freaks, and businessmen of an eerily modern world, rather than the folk heroes and war-bosses of Classical and Archaic antiquity. Among athletes only the boxer would retain his mythic aura in this sinister age of imperial politics and slaughter.

The Ancient Greats

The Author's Ranking of Ancient Prizefighters

Although *monomakhaists* and *gladiators* were prizefighters they are excluded from these lists unless they also competed as *athletes*.

The 10 Most Accomplished Prizefighters of Antiquity

1. Theogenes of Thasos, 476 B.C.: Won more bouts than any fighter.
2. Milo of Kroton, 528 B.C.: The most dominant combat *athlete.*
3. Asklepiades of Alexandria A.D. 180 The most feared combat *athlete.*
4. Klietomakhos of Thebes, 214 B.C.: The best single day in combat sports.
5. Artimodorus of Tralles, A.D. 68: The best tournament showing in history.
6. Dorieus of Rhodes, 436 B.C.: Dominated boxing and *pankration.*
7. Damostratus of Sardis, A.D. 172 Dominated *pankration*, undefeated boxer.
8. Arkhibius of Alexandria A.D. 101 Dominant *pankratiast*, wrestler & boxer.
9. Hipposthenes of Sparta, 620s B.C. Most men's *Olympic* wrestling victories.
10. Kaprus of Elis, 216 B.C.: Won *Olympic* wrestling & *pankration* twice.

The 10 Most Accomplished Boxers of Antiquity

1 Theogenes of Thasos, 476 B.C. : Won more bouts than any boxer*.
2 Tisander of Naxos, 532 B.C.: Won more *Olympics* than any boxer.
3 Melankomas of Karia, A.D. 76: Undefeated, unmarked with gauntlets.
4 Euthymus of Lokri, 480 B.C.: Second best *Olympic* boxer.
5 Glaukos of Karystos, 512 B.C.: Second best *Nemean* & *Isthmian* boxer.
6 Satyrus of Elis, 332 B.C. Dominated early gauntlet boxing
7 Diagoras of Rhodes, 464 B.C.: Dominated classical boxing*.
8 Tullius of Apamea, A.D. 113: Dominant boxer of late antiquity**.
9 Damostratus of Sardis, A.D. 172: Undefeated gauntlet boxer.
10 Klietomakhos of Thebes, 214 B.C.: Craftiest boxer of the Hellenistic Age.

The 10 Most Accomplished *Pankratiasts* of Antiquity

1 Asklepiades of Alexandria, A.D. 180: Was the most feared fighter in history*.

2 Artemidorusof Tralles, A.D. 68: Only boy to defeat boys, youths & men*.

3 Sostratus of Sikyon, 350 B.C.: Most dominant *Olympic pankratiast***.

4 Dorieus of Rhodes, 436 B.C.: Was the most feared classical *pankratiast**.

5 Menander of Aphrodisias, A.D.: 141 Won *Olympics* as boy, youth and man*.

6 Arkhibius of Alexandria A.D. 101: Most versatile of the dominant *pankratiasts**.

7 Damostratus of Sardis, A.D. 172: Most successful boxer/*pankratiast***.

8 Glyko of Pergamon, 100s B.C.: The first to be undefeated on three continents*.

9 Arrakhion of Phigalia, 568 B.C.: Submitted opponent as he himself died.

10 Apollonius of Smyrna, 215 B.C.: Retired as a double *periodinikes***.

The 10 Most Accomplished Wrestlers of Antiquity

1   Milo of Kroton, 528 B.C.: Dominated men's wrestling for 20-24 years**.
2   Hipposthenes of Sparta, 580s B.C.: Dominated men's wrestling for 20-24 years.
3   Hetoemokles of Sparta, 560s B.C.: Dominated men's wrestling for 16-20 years.
4   Khairon of Pellene, 360 B.C.: Dominated men's wrestling for 12-16 years.
5   Pythodelos of Athens, 450 B.C.: Dominated men's wrestling for 12-14 years.
6   Khilon of Patrae, 344 B.C.: Dominated men's wrestling for 6-8 years*.
7   Khrysippus of Smyrna, A.D. 170s *Periodinikes*.
8   Demetrios of Alexandria, A.D. 150s: *Periodinikes*.
9   Aristomenes of Aegina, 444 B.C.: *Periodinikes*.
10   Kaprus of Elis, 212 B.C.: Only two-time "successor of Herakles"

The 10 Most Accomplished Pentathletes of Ancient Hellas

1   Gorgus of Elis, 200s B.C. 4 *Olympic* victories.
2   Antiokhus of Lepreus, 372 B.C.: 2 *Olympic* & 2 *Nemean* victories.
3   Stomius of Elis, 380 B.C.: 1 *Olympic* & 3 *Nemean* victories.
4   Timon of Elis, 200s B.C.: 1 *Olympic* & 1 *Pythian* victory.
5   Aeskhines of Elis, 400s B.C.: 2 *Olympic* victories.
6   Eupolemus of Elis, 400s B.C. 2 *Pythian* & 1 *Nemean* victory.
7   Phaylus of Kroton, 482 B.C.: 2 *Pythian* victories.
8   Hysmon of Elis, 300s? B.C.: 1 *Olympic* & 1 *Nemean* victory.
9   Damiskus of Messene, 200s? B.C.: 1 boy's *Olympic*, 1 *Nemean* & 1 *Isthmian*
10   Theopompus of Argos, 512 B.C.: 1 *Olympic* victory.

Periodinikes is a title originating in the Hellenistic age for a winner of all 4 games of the *periodos* in the same event; a grand-slam so-to-speak sweeping the *Olympian, Nemean, Isthmian*, and *Pythian agons*. This could be done in various ways and seems to have been a cumulative recognition of achievement. Fighters with a ** designation accumulated at least two victories in each *agon* of the *periodos* throughout their careers.

Unique Achievements in Ancient Combat Sports

1. Klietomakhos of Thebes [214 B.C.] won wrestling without a throw, boxing with the gauntlets, *and* the *pankration*, all on a single day at the *Isthmian agon*, thereby gaining the jealousy of the King of Egypt.
2. Artimodorus of Tralles [A.D. 68] who was judged small for a boy [a flyweight], defeated the boys [bantamweights], the youths [featherweights], and the men [lightweights thru heavyweights] in the *pankration* at the Smyrna *agon* over the course of two days.
3. Antiokhus of Lepreus [376-72 B.C.] won crowns in the *Olympic* and *Nemean pentathlon* and in the *Olympic pankration*, making him the most versatile combat

athlete in history.

4. Kaprus of Elis [212-08 B.C.] by winning wrestling and the *pankration* at the same *Olympics* twice, was unmatched as a wrestler/*pankratiast*.

5. Paeanius of Elis [218 B.C.] won the boys boxing at the Pythia [establishing him as a bantamweight or featherweight at best] and went on to defeat the contestants in men's wrestling and men's boxing on the next day. Had he not fought in the shadow of Klietomakhos and Kaprus he may have surpassed Artimodorus as an overachieving underdog.

6. Eutelidas of Sparta [628 B.C.] won the boys *pentathlon* and boys wrestling at the 38th *Olympiad*.

The Rewards

Ancient Money & Modern Equivalents

Babylonian & Persian

Shekel: ¼ ounce of silver or gold

Mina: 60 *shekels*, or 15-16 ounces of silver or gold

Talent: 3600 *shekels*, 60 *mina*, or 60 pounds of silver or gold
   The commoner would measure his wealth in *shekels*, the businessman or local official by *mina*; and kings by the *talent*.

Greek & Hellenistic

Note: Modern equivalents are for the mid-Atlantic region of the United States of America in the year 2005.

Drakhmae: basic unit of exchange; a day's pay for a skilled laborer, about $80-$120; the cost of a pair of quality boots or professional-quality boxing gloves

Obol: 1 6th of a *drakhmae*; jurors were paid by the *obol* for their services, about the cost of a case of premium beer, or a cheap pair of training gloves

Tetradrakhmae: 4 *drakhmae*; issued by Athens and later Makedonia at the height of their military power, perhaps as a convenient denomination for troop payment

Mina: 100 *drakhmae*; approximate cost of a horse, or *hoplite panoply*
    About $8-$12,000; the cost of a good used car or a quality boxing ring

Talent: 60 *mina* or 6,000 *drakhmae*; approximate cost of building a single war-galley
    About $600,000; enough to purchase a suburban mansion

Coins were minted on the Thrakian standard for Balkan transactions or on the Attik (Athenian) standard for larger scale Mediterranean commerce. These coins would often be minted by a ruler and named after him.

The above are values for the classical and Hellenistic period. One should never forget the effects of inflation: by 77 A.D. the price of a horse had risen to 2700 *drakhmae* and by 206 A.D. dancing girls were commanding 12+ *drachmae* a day.

The Risks

Just how dangerous were these activities? Below is a table that compares various risky behavior over the ages.

Longevity is the average career length expressed in years. [I can tell you right off the bat that historians are going to disagree with my calculation for gladiators. Look, half of all gladiators died the first time out. That brings you to 50% before you even start charting a career. First timers did not get a second chance. They got tossed onto the meat wagon.] An act under longevity means that this circumstance is generally an unusual circumstance in that person's life. Monomakhiasts generally only dueled once, for example.

Death percentages are based on the number of people killed out of every 100 engaging in this risky activity. Figures for ancient warrior types are averages, and reflect a lot of information based on Alexander's campaigns and other Greco-Persian conflicts, which were one-sided. When the various types of ancient warriors listed below met in major battles death rates could be astronomical.

Modern figures come from law-enforcement, my violence study conducted from May 1996 to June 2000 [*Logic of Force, Logic of Steel*], and sports literature.

Participant	Longevity	Death%
Common causes of death		
Ancient		
Wrestler	6	2.0
trauma		
Pentathlete	5	2.0
heat-stroke		
Pankratiast	7	1.5
heat-stroke		
Pugmakhiast	6	3.7
heat-stroke, trauma		
Monomakhiast	act	50.0
puncture wounds, lacerations		
Hoplite	30	5.3
puncture wounds		
Phalangite	40	15.0
puncture wounds		
Legionaire	20	12.0
puncture wounds, lacerations		
Gladiator	3	87.5
puncture wounds, lacerations		
Silver miner	1	100.0	heat-stroke, trauma, illness
Modern		
Football player	8	0.3
heat-stroke, trauma		

Motorcyclist trauma	?	0.7	
Scuba diver	?	1.1	?
Boxer trauma	4	0.1	
Jockey trauma	?	12.8	
Hang glider trauma	?	5.6	
Sky diver trauma	?	12.6	
Death row inmate variable [compare to gladiator*]	14	?	
Gang-stabbing victim puncture wounds	act	67.0	
KO'd crime victim trauma	act	16.0	

*A death row inmate will outlive 4 gladiators and 13 ancient silver miners!

Map 8.

The hand-struggling-ground, or wrestling-school, called a palaestra or palaistra. This was a typical facility in a Hellenic community, and eventually at contest sites; where many of the terms illuminated above would have been used.

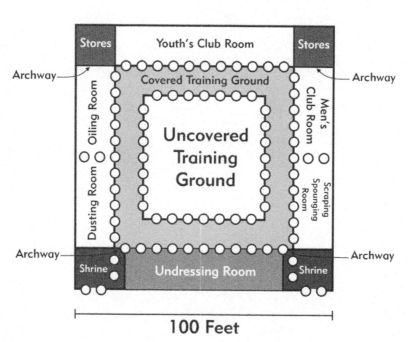

O Pillared Colonnades

The Broken Dance is to be Concluded in
The Boxer Dread

Made in the USA
Monee, IL
26 March 2022

93590344R00128